Be prepared...
To learn...
To succeed...

Get **REA**dy. It all starts here. REA's preparation for the ISAT is **fully aligned** with the Learning Standards adopted by the Illinois State Board of Education.

Visit us online at
www.rea.com

READY, SET, GO!

Illinois
ISAT
Grade 8
Reading

Staff of Research & Education Association

Research & Education Association
Visit our website at
www.rea.com

The Learning Standards in this book were created and implemented by the Illinois State Board of Education (ISBE). For further information, visit the ISBE website at *http://www.isbe.net/assessment/isat.*

"Margaret Murie" photo (p. 15) by Associated Press.
"Space Colonization" photo (p. 218) courtesy NASA.

Research & Education Association
61 Ethel Road West
Piscataway, New Jersey 08854
E-mail: info@rea.com

Ready, Set, Go!
ISAT Reading, Grade 8

Printed in the United States of America

Library of Congress Control Number 2006924964

International Standard Book Number 0-7386-0099-7

 REA® is a registered trademark of
Research & Education Association, Inc.

TABLE OF CONTENTS

Foreword

Since the inception and implementation of the No Child Left Behind legislation, students, teachers, and administrators have become increasingly aware of their responsibility to demonstrate adequate yearly progress as they influence the future workforce of this country. At present, the most efficient method of measuring educational progress is through tests chosen and administered by each state. The State of Illinois currently uses the Illinois Standards Achievement Test (ISAT) as a measure of the progress of eighth grade students. This book provides students with a practical, purposeful, and enjoyable preparation for the reading assessment component of the ISAT.

Students will benefit from using this book to prepare for the ISAT, not only because it offers a comprehensive review of critical reading skills, but also because they will enjoy the high-interest multicultural selections written by both classical and contemporary authors writing in a wide variety of genres. The format of the book directs students to examine their purposes for reading each selection, as well as the relevance of the types of questions used for each selection. Introductory statements of pertinent Illinois State Learning Standards are addressed in an analysis of each question and answer showing the relevance of the exercise to the ISAT.

As students complete the exercises in this book, they will become familiar with the ISAT testing format through analysis of the purpose, content, and structure of the test questions. Explanations of answers to the questions provide valuable practice in using high-level thinking skills such as inference and evaluation. The book teaches students the necessary strategies for comprehension and analysis of the selections and questions. Students using the exercises in this book will develop the confidence and skills needed to master the reading component of the ISAT. These skills will transfer to their daily classroom work and enable the students to become accomplished thinkers and readers. From my experience as an English teacher, this text should be required reading.

Marjorie Jordan, M.S.

Marjorie Jordan has 26 years of experience teaching English in the state of Illinois. She earned a B.S. in Education from the University of Illinois and an M.S. in Technology in Training and Development from Eastern Illinois University.

About Research & Education Association

Founded in 1959, Research & Education Association is dedicated to publishing the finest and most effective educational materials—including software, study guides, and test preps—for students in middle school, high school, college, graduate school, and beyond. Today, REA's wide-ranging catalog is a leading resource for teachers, students, and professionals.

We invite you to visit us at *www.rea.com* to find out how "REA is making the world smarter."

Acknowledgments

We would like to thank Larry B. Kling, Vice President, Editorial, for his editorial direction; Pam Weston, Vice President, Publishing, for setting the quality standards for production integrity and managing the publication to completion; Christine Reilley, Senior Editor, for project management; Diane Goldschmidt, Associate Editor, for post-production quality assurance; Christine Saul, Senior Graphic Artist, for cover design; Jeremy Rech, Graphic Artist, for interior page design; and Jeff LoBalbo, Senior Graphic Artist, for post-production file mapping.

We also gratefully acknowledge the writers, educators, and editors of REA, Northeast Editing, and Publication Services for content development, editorial guidance, and final review.

SUCCEEDING ON THE ISAT— GRADE 8 READING

ABOUT THIS BOOK

This book provides excellent preparation for the Illinois Standards Achievement Test (ISAT)— Grade 8 Reading. Inside you will find exercises designed to provide students with the instruction, practice, and strategies needed to do well on this achievement test.

This book is divided into several parts: a **pretest**, which introduces students to the sections on the actual test, including

- Session 1: six short passages with 30 multiple-choice questions

- Session 2: one long passage with 16 multiple-choice questions and 1 extended-response question, and one short passage with 4 multiple-choice questions

- Session 3: one longer passage with 14 multiple-choice questions and 1 extended-response question

Following the pretest is a lesson section, which teaches students about the different types of ISAT questions on the reading test, step by step. Students will begin with shorter selections and easier questions and conclude each lesson by completing full-length selections and questions modeled after those on the ISAT. Answer explanations are provided for each question in each lesson. "Tips" are also given below each question to guide students toward answering the question correctly. Finally, this book includes a full-length **posttest**, which matches the ISAT test exactly in terms of content.

Begin by assigning students the pretest. Answers and answer explanations follow the pretest. Then work through each of the lessons one by one. When students have completed the book, they should complete the posttest. Answers and answer explanations follow the posttest.

HOW TO USE THIS BOOK

FOR STUDENTS: To make getting through the book as easy as possible, we've included icons shown on the next page that highlight sections like lessons, questions, and answers. You'll find that our practice tests are very much like the actual ISAT you'll encounter on test day. The best way to prepare for a test is to practice, so we've included drills with answers throughout the book, and our two practice tests include detailed answers.

FOR PARENTS: Illinois has created grade-appropriate learning standards that are listed in the table in this introduction. Students need to meet these objectives as measured by the ISAT. Our book will help your child review for the ISAT and prepare for the Reading exam. It includes review sections, drills, and two practice tests complete with explanations to help your child focus on the areas he/she needs to work on to help master the test.

FOR TEACHERS: No doubt, you are already familiar with the ISAT and its format. Begin by assigning students the pretest. An answer key and detailed explanations follow the pretest. Then work through each of the lessons in succession. When students have completed the subject review, they should move on to the posttest. Answers and answer explanations follow the posttest.

ICONS EXPLAINED

Icons make navigating through the book easier by highlighting sections like lessons, questions, and answers as explained below:

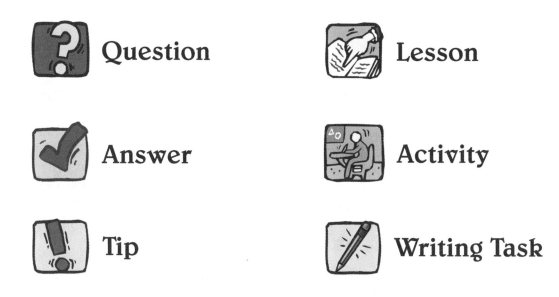

Question   Lesson

Answer   Activity

Tip   Writing Task

WHY STUDENTS ARE REQUIRED TO TAKE THE ISAT

ISAT measures the extent to which students are meeting the Illinois Learning Standards. Illinois teachers and curriculum experts developed the ISAT in cooperation with the Illinois State Board of Education. The reading test is given to students in Grades 3, 5, and 8.

The reading tests in Grade 8 are given in three 45-minute sessions. One of these sessions consists of a passage with 20–25 multiple-choice questions. The other two reading sessions each include one passage with 15–20 multiple-choice questions and one extended-response question.

WHAT'S ON THE ISAT

Reading Selections

Reading selections on the ISAT can be fiction or nonfiction informational. While most reading passages are at or near grade level, about twenty-five percent of the passages are at a lower reading level.

Reading Questions

Most questions on the ISAT are multiple-choice. Both multiple-choice and open-ended questions are based on the Illinois Learning Standards, which are listed below. The first number on each standard refers to the state goal. The second number indicates the grade level, and the third number is the number of the specific objective.

ISAT READING LEARNING STANDARDS*

Standard 1A: Apply word analysis and vocabulary skills to comprehend selections.

		Page Numbers
1.8.01	Determine the meaning of an unknown word using word or content-area vocabulary using knowledge of prefixes, suffixes, and word roots.	59
1.8.02	Use etymologies to determine the meanings of words.	59
1.8.03	Determine the meaning of an unknown word using word, sentence, and cross-sentence clues.	59
1.8.04	Determine the connotation of a word using word, sentence, and cross-sentence clues.	59
1.8.05	Determine the meaning of a word in context when the word has multiple meanings.	59

---

* The Learning Standards in this table were created and implemented by the Illinois State Board of Education (ISBE). For further information, visit the ISBE website at *http://www.isbe.net/assessment/isat.htm*.

Standard 1B: Apply reading strategies to improve understanding and fluency.

Standard 1C: Comprehend a wide range of reading materials.

Standard 2A: Read and understand literature representative of various societies, eras, and ideas.

TIPS FOR THE STUDENT

Students can do plenty of things before and during the actual test to improve their test-taking performance. The good thing is that most of the tips described in the following pages are easy!

Preparing for the Test

Test Anxiety

Do you get nervous when your teacher talks about taking a test? A certain amount of anxiety is normal and it actually may help you prepare better for the test by getting you motivated. But too much anxiety is a bad thing and may keep you from properly preparing for the test. Here are some things to consider that may help relieve test anxiety:

- Share how you are feeling with your parents and your teachers. They may have ways of helping you deal with how you are feeling.

- Keep on top of your game. Are you behind in your homework and class assignments? A lot of your classwork-related anxiety and stress will simply go away if you keep up with your homework assignments and classwork. And then you can focus on the test with a clearer mind.

- Relax. Take a deep breath or two. You should do this especially if you get anxious while taking the test.

Study Tips & Taking the Test

- **Learn the Test's Format.** Don't be surprised. By taking a practice test ahead of time you'll know what the test looks like, how much time you will have, how many questions there are, and what kinds of questions are going to appear on it. Knowing ahead of time is much better than being surprised.

- **Read the Entire Question.** Pay attention to what kind of answer a question or word problem is looking for. Reread the question if it does not make sense to you, and try to note the parts of the question needed for figuring out the right answer.

- **Read All the Answers.** On a multiple-choice test, the right answer could also be the last answer. You won't know unless you read all the possible answers to a question.

- **It's Not a Guessing Game.** If you don't know the answer to a question, don't make an uneducated guess. And don't randomly pick just any answer either. As you read over each possible answer to a question, note any answers which are obviously wrong. Each obviously wrong answer you identify and eliminate greatly improves your chances at selecting the right answer.

- **Don't Get Stuck on Questions.** Don't spend too much time on any one question. Doing this takes away time from the other questions. Work on the easier questions first. Skip the really hard questions and come back to them if there is still enough time.

- **Accuracy Counts.** Make sure you record your answer in the correct space on your answer sheet. Fixing mistakes only takes time away from you.

- **Finished Early?** Use this time wisely and double-check your answers.

Sound Advice for Test Day

The Night Before. Getting a good night's rest keeps your mind sharp and focused for the test.

The Morning of the Test. Have a good breakfast. Dress in comfortable clothes. Keep in mind that you don't want to be too hot or too cold while taking the test. Get to school on time. Give yourself time to gather your thoughts and calm down before the test begins.

Three Steps for Taking the Test

1) **Read.** Read the entire question and then read all the possible answers.

2) **Answer.** Answer the easier questions first and then go back to the more difficult questions.

3) **Double-Check.** Go back and check your work if time permits.

TIPS FOR PARENTS

- Encourage your child to take responsibility for homework and class assignments. Help your child create a study schedule. Mark the test's date on a family calendar as a reminder for both of you.

- Talk to your child's teachers. Ask them for progress reports on an ongoing basis.

- Commend your child's study and test successes. Praise your child for successfully following a study schedule, for doing homework, and for any work done well.

- Test Anxiety. Your child may experience nervousness or anxiety about the test. You may even be anxious, too. Here are some helpful tips on dealing with a child's test anxiety:

  - Talk about the test openly and positively with your child. An ongoing dialogue not only can relieve your child's anxieties but also serves as a progress report of how your child feels about the test.

  - Form realistic expectations of your child's testing abilities.

  - Be a "Test Cheerleader." Your encouragement to do his or her best on the test can alleviate your child's test anxiety.

Session 1

Now read this passage and answer the questions that follow. You will have forty-five minutes to complete this session.

Ansel Adams: Photographer and Conservationist

1   Ansel Adams was a famous photographer known for capturing the magnificent beauty of western landscapes in his photographs. Born in San Francisco, California, on February 20, 1902, Adams attended school until eighth grade. He was then taught at home by his father and several tutors. Adams took an early interest in music, teaching himself to play the piano and later studying with a professor. He was incredibly talented, and, for a long time, he considered a career as a professional musician.

2   In 1916, Adams vacationed with his family in Yosemite National Park in California. Armed with a camera, a gift from his parents, Adams took pictures of the beautiful scenery in the park. The trip to Yosemite and the pictures he took introduced Adams to the beauty of nature and the outdoors. He continued to visit Yosemite once a year. He documented the wonderful wilderness that surrounded him. In 1919, Adams joined the Sierra Club, an organization dedicated to enjoying and preserving forests in the Pacific region, specifically in the Sierra Nevada Mountains. Adams later went on to serve as president of the organization.

3   Adams continued his music studies, taking pictures only as a hobby. But his photographs were consistently appreciated, leading Adams to publish two books of his photographs. Adams subsequently decided to focus on a career in photography. In 1930, Adams met photographer Paul Strand. Adams admired Strand's pictures for their clear, sharp images, which contrasted with the softer style popular at that time.

4   In 1937, Adams moved to the Yosemite Valley. Using Strand's "straight-photography," Adams began publishing books of his beautiful pictures including *Illustrated Guide to Yosemite Valley* and *Yosemite and the High Sierra*. The more time Adams spent surrounded by the beauty of Yosemite and the Sierra Nevada, the more concerned he became with the environment. He felt strongly about preserving the wilderness. In his years with the Sierra Club, he spoke often about conservation and preservation.

5   Adams died on April 22, 1984, but his incredible photographs are still admired today. Shortly after his death, Congress designated more than 229,000 acres of land as the Ansel Adams Wilderness Area and a mountain in his beloved Yosemite Valley was named after him a year later.

GO ON ▶

1

Why did the author most likely write this passage?

A To convince readers that preserving wilderness is important

B To explain how to take pictures of nature scenes

C To entertain readers with a story about a famous American figure

D To describe the life and career of a famous photographer

2

The passage says that Adams published two books of photography and <u>subsequently</u> decided to focus on a career in photography. What does <u>subsequently</u> mean?

A Reluctantly

B Afterward

C Intelligently

D Changeable

3

What was most likely the reason that a large portion of Yosemite Valley was named after Ansel Adams?

A Adams owned and lived on the land and did not want it to be sold.

B Congress did not want people to disturb the place where Adams once lived.

C People wanted to pay tribute to Adams and his love of the land.

D The Sierra Club wanted to preserve the land for their organization.

4

Which of the following is the best summary of the second paragraph of the passage?

A Adams' parents are credited with starting his career in nature photography.

B Adams' desire to visit other places faded after his first trip to Yosemite National Park.

C Adams' time in the Yosemite National Park inspired him to become a protector of nature.

D Adams' main goal was to protect and conserve forests in the Pacific region.

5

How did Adams probably feel when he met photographer Paul Strand?

A Skeptical
B Inspired
C Jealous
D Intimidated

Now read this passage and answer the questions that follow.

Excerpt from *Hard Times*
CHAPTER I — THE ONE THING NEEDFUL
by Charles Dickens

1   'NOW, what I want is, Facts. Teach these boys and girls nothing but Facts. Facts alone are wanted in life. Plant nothing else, and root out everything else. You can only form the minds of reasoning animals upon Facts: nothing else will ever be of any service to them. This is the principle on which I bring up my own children, and this is the principle on which I bring up these children. Stick to Facts, sir!'

2   The scene was a plain, bare, monotonous vault of a school-room, and the speaker's square forefinger emphasized his observations by underscoring every sentence with a line on the schoolmaster's sleeve. The emphasis was helped by the speaker's square wall of a forehead, which had his eyebrows for its base, while his eyes found commodious cellarage in two dark caves, overshadowed by the wall. The emphasis was helped by the speaker's mouth, which was wide, thin, and hard set. The emphasis was helped by the speaker's voice, which was inflexible, dry, and dictatorial. The emphasis was helped by the speaker's hair, which bristled on the skirts of his bald head, a plantation of firs to keep the wind from its shining surface, all covered with knobs, like the crust of a plum pie, as if the head had scarcely warehouse-room for the hard facts stored inside. The speaker's obstinate carriage, square coat, square legs, square shoulders,—nay, his very neckcloth, trained to take him by the throat with an unaccommodating grasp, like a stubborn fact, as it was,—all helped the emphasis.

3   'In this life, we want nothing but Facts, sir; nothing but Facts!'

4   The speaker, and the schoolmaster, and the third grown person present, all backed a little, and swept with their eyes the inclined plane of little vessels then and there arranged in order, ready to have imperial gallons of facts poured into them until they were full to the brim.

GO ON ▶

6 Which words best describe the mood of this passage?

A   Sad and serious
B   Tense and uncomfortable
C   Quiet and calm
D   Exciting and adventurous

7 Why does the speaker repeat the word "facts"?

A   to scare the students
B   to give the students information
C   to stress his point
D   to clear up any confusion

8 What can you conclude about the speaker's relationship to the others in the passage?

A   He is the students' teacher.
B   He is someone of high authority.
C   He is a parent of one of the students.
D   He is a friend of the schoolmaster.

9 The passage says that the characters stepped back to look at the inclined plane of little vessels. What does the author mean by inclined plane of little vessels?

A   the students in their seats
B   the hair on the speaker's head
C   the teachers in the room
D   the speaker's square forehead

10 The passage "Hard Times" is an example of which type of literature?

A   Biography
B   Fiction
C   Essay
D   Myth

GO ON ▶

Now read this passage and answer the questions that follow.

Unearthing Mysteries of the Dead Sea Scrolls

1   In 1947, a group of shepherds searching for a lost goat in the Judean Desert stumbled upon something amazing. They entered a deep cave that had been untouched for many years and discovered pottery jars containing parchment-paper scrolls—seven in all. While these shepherds could not decipher the information conveyed on the scrolls, they speculated that they were very old and of great value.

2   The shepherds sold the scrolls to someone, who sold them to someone else. The scrolls eventually caught the attention of American and European scholars, who identified them as ancient writings from people who once lived in Qumran (pronounced: koom-rahn), an ancient city near the Dead Sea, which is located in Israel and Jordan about fifteen miles east of Jerusalem.

3   About two years after the shepherds discovered the scrolls, archaeologists pinpointed the cave in which they were found and they dubbed this cave "Qumran Cave 1." Upon further exploration, archaeologists discovered additional scrolls in Cave 1 as well as fragments from scrolls dating back to 200 B.C.E. to 68 C.E. They also found pottery as well as cloth and wood. These findings proved the authenticity of the documents and helped to broaden excavation in the area. Archaeologists unearthed other caves containing scrolls and fragments, which led to the excavation (digging out) of Qumran in the 1950s. Approximately 900 scrolls, most of which were fragments, were discovered by archeologists and others in eleven caves near Qumran.

4   What information is on the scrolls? They contain mostly religious myths and hymns. Archaeologists believe that the scrolls once comprised the library of a group of radical Jewish people, who hid in caves around the outbreak of the Jewish-Roman War (66 C.E.), but whose ancestors may have been living in and around these caves as early as 150 B.C.E. The group, dubbed the "Dead Sea Sect," was intensely religious, conservative, and "hermit-like," rarely if ever socializing with others of their time. But not all of what was found of the Dead Sea Scrolls was religious in nature.

5   One of the most mysterious manuscripts found is known as the Copper Scroll. Discovered in 1952 in what came to be known as Cave 3, it is one of the only scrolls to be found by archaeologists. The Copper Scroll was found in its original resting place, where it was placed almost two thousand years earlier. Long ago information was engraved onto thin sheets of copper. Then the sheets of copper were joined together. When the Copper Scroll was found, it had been rolled into a scroll that over time had become too fragile to unroll. For a long time, experts suggested ways to open the scroll without destroying any of the information. Using a very small saw, they cut the scroll into thirty-two slivers, each one curved into the shape of the scroll. Finally, they could interpret the important message.

GO ON ▶

6   The first column of the Copper Scroll begins, "In the fortress which is in the Vale of Achor, forty cubits under the steps entering to the east: a money chest and it [sic] contents, of a weight of seventeen talents." The scroll revealed evidence of buried treasure, a huge collection of gold, silver, and other valuables worth more than one million dollars. No one has claimed the treasure yet. Much of the information on the scrolls hasn't been translated or understood. Many people wonder to whom the treasure may have belonged. Others suggest there is no treasure, just a very old work of fiction.

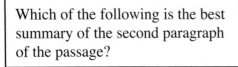

11

Which of the following is the best summary of the second paragraph of the passage?

A The Dead Sea is about fifteen miles east of Jerusalem.

B European and American scholars worked together to figure out who created the scrolls.

C The scrolls traveled through many hands until their origin was discovered.

D The shepherds sold the original scrolls instead of keeping them.

12

According to the passage, why did archaeologists decide to excavate Qumran?

A They found many historical materials in Qumran Cave 1.

B They heard that shepherds had discovered many scrolls in the area.

C They wanted to figure out what information the scrolls contained.

D They knew that the Dead Sea Sect had hidden religious information in the ancient city.

13

Which word best describes the mood of the first paragraph of the passage?

A Mysterious
B Resentful
C Elated
D Indifferent

14

The passage says that archaeologists found the caves that the shepherds discovered and <u>dubbed</u> it "Qumran Cave 1." What does <u>dubbed</u> mean?

A Understood
B Named
C Considered
D Replaced

15

The passage "Unearthing Mysteries of the Dead Sea Scrolls" is an example of which type of literature?

A Legend
B Drama
C Nonfiction
D Fairy tale

GO ON ▶

Now read this passage and answer the questions that follow.

Memories of Montgomery
by Evelyn Smith

1   Growing up as a black child in Montgomery, Alabama, in the 1950s was challenging, and it taught me some valuable lessons. Unfortunately, most lessons learned during this time were taught the hard way, which seemed to be the only way. During the earliest part of my childhood, most whites in Montgomery essentially pretended that my family and others like us did not exist. We sat in the rear of the bus, did not dine in restaurants, and occupied separate waiting rooms everywhere we went. As a child I did not question these practices because I had never yearned for an equal world. My parents, however, longed for things to improve.

2   It was December 1, 1955—I was six—when a woman named Rosa Parks refused to give up her seat to a white man on a Montgomery bus. Suddenly, my parents would no longer allow us to travel on Montgomery public transportation. I didn't understand the reasoning behind it, but I knew that racial conflict in Montgomery was getting severe. Our pastor, Pastor Vernon, organized a car pool for the blacks in our neighborhood so that we wouldn't have to furnish money to the city by using public transportation. One day, on our way to school, an enraged white man smashed the car's windshield with the tip of his cane. I was never so frightened, and that was when I realized the consuming nature of foolish hatred—his, not my own. A week later, after my mother started to walk me to school, Pastor Vernon was arrested while driving that same car. The officers said he was speeding, but Pastor Vernon insisted that he wasn't, and I knew that he wouldn't lie.

3   All through that winter I walked to school, ignoring the glares of the whites as we passed, playing word games with my mother to forget about hatred, about

GO ON ▶

the reasons we were walking, the reasons I was beginning to understand. When my mother read of bombings and riots in the paper she would let me stay home from school. At first I was delighted to stay home, but then I began to recognize the terror in my mother's eyes, and I felt like a prisoner, wondering if I would ever ride the bus again. Then, on November 13, 1956, the Supreme Court ruled that segregation on public buses in Montgomery was illegal. On my eighth birthday, my mother and I sat directly behind the driver, and though the dangers were not over, this was a very happy memory for me because it was the first time I felt like we were winning against hate.

GO ON ▶

16 Which words would the author most likely use to describe her childhood in Montgomery?

A Chaotic but satisfying
B Upsetting and gloomy
C Enjoyable but boring
D Exciting and thrilling

17 According to the passage, when were the author and her mother finally allowed to sit at the front of the bus?

A When Rosa Parks refused to give up her seat for a white man
B When a stranger in Montgomery smashed Pastor Vernon's windshield with the tip of his cane
C When the American government stated that segregation on Montgomery public buses was illegal
D When bombings and riots started to occur in Montgomery

18 The passage "Memories of Montgomery" is an example of which type of literature?

A Historical fiction
B Folktale
C Autobiography
D Poetry

19 The author writes that her pastor took her to school so that her family would not have to <u>furnish</u> money to the city. What does <u>furnish</u> mean?

A Waste
B Supply
C Decorate
D Spend

20 Why did the author most likely write this passage?

A To entertain with a funny story about growing up in Montgomery
B To explain why she hated her childhood
C To illustrate what it was like to grow up in a segregated city
D To show why she now loves sitting at the front of the bus

Now read this passage and answer the questions that follow.

Margaret Murie, Daughter of Alaska

1   Margaret Murie was one of the greatest preservationists of the twentieth century. A preservationist is someone who dedicates his or her life to preserving parts of the world, so these places stay clean, healthy, and undisturbed by humankind's often-destructive influence.

2   Margaret Elizabeth Thomas was born on August 18, 1902, in Seattle, Washington. As a young girl she moved to Fairbanks, Alaska, and quickly developed a lifelong love of the Alaskan wilderness. It was there that she began her distinguished career. In 1924 she became the first woman to graduate from the University of Alaska. During this time she also met and married naturalist Olaus Murie, who shared her passion for Alaska. The couple even spent their honeymoon on a 550-mile dogsled expedition!

3   The Muries soon had children and the family lived together in Alaska, where they became accustomed to taking months-long treks into the wilderness. Olaus worked for the Biological Survey, and as part of his job, he studied the many plants and animals he observed during these trips. Margaret wrote a book about their unique adventures.

4   Although their love for Alaska never faded, the Murie family decided to move to Wyoming in 1926. They took up residence in a log cabin and studied the elk of the forests. During that time, they initiated a crusade of letters and lectures to convince the nation's leaders to protect wilderness areas. They didn't want to see nature's splendor disappear under oil-drilling rigs or highways, or be destroyed by logging companies. Thanks to their efforts, thousands of miles of wilderness areas were designated as wildlife refuge areas, where animals and plants were protected by law.

5   Though Olaus died in 1963, Margaret, often called "Mardy" by close friends, continued her efforts to preserve the land that she loved. The next year she joined President Lyndon B. Johnson at the signing of the Wilderness Act, which allowed the National Wilderness Preservation System (NWPS) to select pieces of land in need of protection. As of 1998, the NWPS has been given the task of protecting many millions of acres of land. After this trip, Margaret once again focused her attention on her beloved Alaska. She even spoke before Congress about the importance of keeping Alaska free from exploitation. She believed that the value of Alaska itself was greater than any moneymaking resources like oil or gold that might be found there. She said, "Beauty is a resource in and of itself. Alaska must be allowed to be Alaska; that is her greatest economy. I hope the United States of America is not so rich that she can afford to let these wildernesses pass by, or so poor she cannot afford to keep them."

6   Margaret's message hit home, and in 1980, the Alaska Lands Act was signed by President Jimmy Carter. This act greatly expanded the size of the NWPS, America's national parks, and the National Wildlife Refuge System. It

GO ON ▶

promised to keep large sections of land clean and free for future generations to enjoy. Margaret was thrilled and relieved to see these safeguards introduced. She wrote, "when the oil and the minerals have all been found and taken away, the one hundred million acres of national parks and refuges and wild rivers and forests will be the most beneficent treasure in [Alaska.] I would plead with all administrators, 'Please allow Alaska to be different, to be herself, to nourish our souls.'"

7   In her later years, Margaret dedicated her time not only to societies and councils that watched over America's natural resources, but also opened the Teton Science School. Here students of all ages are taught about ecology, which is the relationship between plants and animals and their environment.

8   In January, 1998, Margaret was again summoned by a president. This time it was President Bill Clinton, who awarded her the Medal of Freedom for her dedication to conservation. Clinton said, "We owe much to the life's work of Mardy Murie, a pioneer of the environmental movement, who, with her husband Olaus, helped set the course of American conservation more than seventy years ago." Though Margaret passed away five years later at the age of 101, her contributions live on.

GO ON ▶

21

According to the passage, why did Margaret and her husband write letters to the American government?

A To ask for funds for Margaret to write a book about their adventures

B To request permission to speak in front of Congress about the Alaska Lands Act

C To thank President Bill Clinton for their Medal of Freedom

D To convince American government to protect wilderness areas

22

Which of the following is the best summary of the sixth paragraph of this passage?

A President Jimmy Carter passed the Alaska Lands Act in 1980.

B Margaret's hard work led to the passing of the 1980 Alaska Lands Act, which protected large amounts of American land.

C Margaret pleaded with government officials to leave Alaskan lands untouched because they were good for Americans' souls.

D President Jimmy Carter expanded the amount of area reserved for America's national parks.

23

According to the passage, why did Margaret want Alaskan lands to be designated as wildlife refuge areas?

A So the plants and animals in these areas would be protected

B So the nation would stop using so much oil

C So her children would have safe and beautiful places to play

D So her husband would have a place to do his work

24

According to the passage, President Bill Clinton referred to Margaret as a "pioneer of the environmental movement." What does this mean?

A Margaret and her family traveled through the Alaskan wilderness in a dogsled.

B Margaret was one of the first people to push the government to protect wilderness areas.

C Margaret was very rugged and could have easily survived during the settling of America.

D Margaret discovered many areas that no one knew even existed.

GO ON ▶

25

What can you conclude about
Margaret from the passage?

A She was funny and goofy.
B She was loving and warm.
C She was fragile and gentle.
D She was selfless and dedicated.

Now read this passage and answer the questions that follow.

Chicago Poet
(from Cornhuskers, Henry Holt, 1918)
by Carl Sandburg

I saluted a nobody.
I saw him in a looking-glass.
He smiled—so did I.
He crumpled the skin on his forehead, frowning—so did I.
5   Everything I did he did.
I said, "Hello, I know you."
And I was a liar to say so.

Ah, this looking-glass man!
Liar, fool, dreamer, play-actor,
10   Soldier, dusty drinker of dust—
Ah! he will go with me
Down the dark stairway
When nobody else is looking,
When everybody else is gone.

15   He locks his elbow in mine,
I lose all—but not him.

GO ON ▶

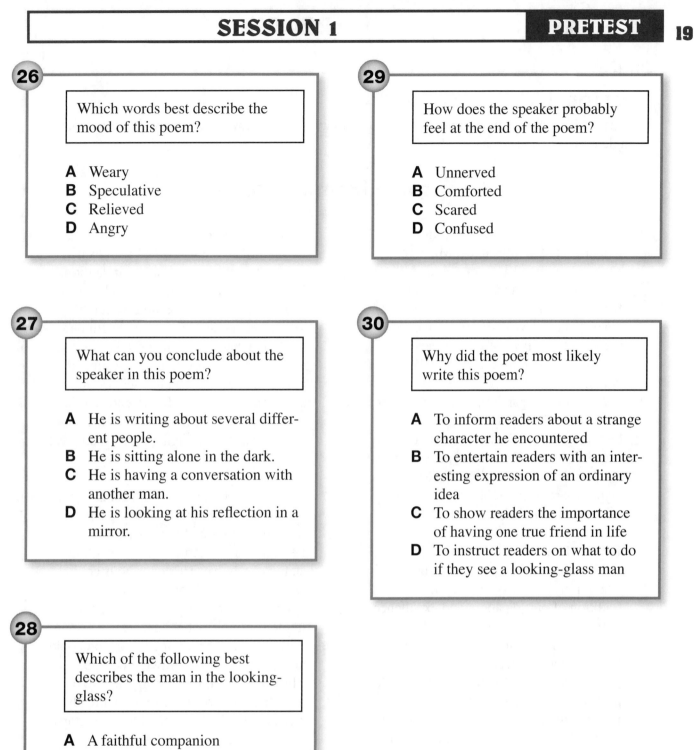

26 Which words best describe the mood of this poem?

A Weary
B Speculative
C Relieved
D Angry

29 How does the speaker probably feel at the end of the poem?

A Unnerved
B Comforted
C Scared
D Confused

27 What can you conclude about the speaker in this poem?

A He is writing about several different people.
B He is sitting alone in the dark.
C He is having a conversation with another man.
D He is looking at his reflection in a mirror.

30 Why did the poet most likely write this poem?

A To inform readers about a strange character he encountered
B To entertain readers with an interesting expression of an ordinary idea
C To show readers the importance of having one true friend in life
D To instruct readers on what to do if they see a looking-glass man

28 Which of the following best describes the man in the looking-glass?

A A faithful companion
B An enthusiastic teacher
C A brave warrior
D A foolish idealist

STOP

Session 2

Now read this passage and answer the questions that follow. You will have forty-five minutes to complete this session.

A Horse from History

1   What do Renaissance Italy and modern-day Grand Rapids, Michigan, have in common? This may sound like the beginning of a very strange riddle. However, it only becomes stranger when the answer is revealed: The connection between these two different times and places is *Il Cavallo*, the world's largest horse!

2   *Il Cavallo* began long ago in the mind of the remarkable Renaissance artist Leonardo da Vinci and now resides in Frederik Meijer Botanical and Sculpture Gardens in Grand Rapids. The Sculpture Gardens are open to the public—you can stop by and say hello to the horse!

Leonardo: A Man of Vision

3   Leonardo da Vinci was born in 1452 in Vinci, Italy. The city of Vinci had a long tradition of participation, and excellence, in the arts. Early in Leonardo's life, he involved himself in this tradition by becoming an apprentice to a renowned painter, Andrea del Verrochio. Leonardo proved his skill and vision almost immediately. Before he even turned 20, Leonardo was outdoing his master. In one instance, he was assigned to paint a figure in one of Verrochio's paintings; Leonardo's contribution to the painting was so much better than Verrochio's, the old master gave up painting for good.

4   In order to fund further art projects, Leonardo went to work for Duke Ludovico Sforza of Milan. During this time, Leonardo began producing the amazing artwork that would earn him a place in history. The Duke employed Leonardo's artistic skills as well as his hidden talents for design and invention. Leonardo designed castles, machines, and even weapons for his ambitious employer. To fuel his creativity, Leonardo studied math, mechanics, architecture, anatomy, warfare, and nature. The well-rounded education he provided himself would serve him well in his future endeavors, and help prepare him for one of the Duke's most challenging assignments yet.

The History

5   Over five hundred years ago, Ludovico Sforza hired Leonardo to tackle an incredible project. Sforza wanted Leonardo to construct the world's largest statue of a horse. This enormous equine would be cast in bronze and would stand, twenty-four feet tall, near his palatial home in the city of Milan.

6   Leonardo took up one of his notebooks and sketched a tiny drawing of a horse. This first drawing was only the size of a postage stamp, but Leonardo already realized that he loved the idea. The horse would be a symbol of strength, beauty, and peace. He set about studying and sketching horses, planning one of the most striking statues of all time.

7   After countless hours of preparation, Leonardo began constructing a full-size model of the horse out of clay. This was the first step in the process of casting a bronze statue; however, the rest of the process would never take place. During a war, French soldiers captured the palace

GO ON ▶

of Duke Sforza. When they saw the huge clay horse, they drew their crossbows and began firing arrows at it. They used the clay model for target practice until it was damaged beyond repair.

8   Leonardo's work was ruined, and his dream was lost. Some stories hold that he regretted this for the rest of his life, loathing the mention of it because its memory was too painful. Some lore suggests he even wept on his deathbed over the loss of the horse. Regardless, Leonardo's *Il Cavallo* was never completed, and the entire idea went nearly forgotten for centuries.

Rebirth of the Dream

9   In 1978, a Pennsylvanian pilot and sculptor named Charles C. Dent read an article about Leonardo's vision for *Il Cavallo*—a name that simply means "The Horse." Dent was fascinated and quickly began an endeavor to sculpt a replica of the horse using Leonardo's blueprints. Then, as his enthusiasm grew, Dent began making plans to have a full-size statue constructed. Not only did he want to make Leonardo's vision a reality, but he also wanted to honor the people and history of Italy. He would make the horse a gift to them.

10   This would be a giant project, and Dent knew he couldn't do it alone. He helped to gather a foundation of people willing to donate time and money to the lofty goal. When Dent died in 1994, the foundation continued his work and invested millions of dollars and thousands of hours into the project. Scholars, artists, metal specialists, sponsors, and even animal experts worked together to develop a statue that would do Leonardo honor.

Building a Reality

11   After the workers had made their plans, they built an eight-foot model of the horse they hoped to build. Then they used special enlarging machines to increase the size of the horse to a huge twenty-four feet. Finally, the most demanding part of the project was handed over to workers at a foundry, or metal-working shop. They put in many months of patient labor to cast the approximately sixty small bronze parts of the giant statue.

12   The bronze was cast in thin sheets that would serve as the statue's "skin." Since they were too thin to hold up the weight of the assembled statue, the foundry workers had to reinforce the sheets with a heavy "skeleton" underneath them. Later still, the workers would have to attach the sheets to the supports, and then join them all together in a beautiful and seamless fashion.

13   When they completed this, however, the result was astonishing: a fifteen-ton bronze steed, taller than a house! As soon as it was done, thousands of people flocked to see it. This horse was not meant to be kept in its stable, however; it was instead shipped to Milan, Italy. In 1999, *Il Cavallo* was set up in a cultural park for all the people of the city to enjoy. It stood right where Leonardo and Sforza might have placed theirs, if it hadn't been destroyed by war.

14   But the story doesn't end there. Seeing that so much work had been invested in the single statue, some people decided to make a second one using the same molds and tools. This identical twin horse would be kept in America—Frederik Meijer Gardens in Grand Rapids, Michigan, to be exact. On October 7, 1999, this *Il Cavallo* was unveiled as part of a joyous ceremony in which bands, jugglers, and Renaissance re-enactors celebrated the new life brought to the dreams of Leonardo da Vinci. Leonardo's horse, the noteworthy symbol of peace and strength, would ride again!

Il Cavallo Quick Facts

Height: 24 feet
Weight: 15 tons
Composed of silicon bronze, with skeleton of stainless steel
Construction began around 1980
Unveiled on October 7, 1999
Location: Frederik Meijer Botanical and Sculpture Gardens, Grand Rapids, Michigan.
Stands near an educational center which includes an identical *Il Cavallo* in 1/3 scale

GO ON ▶

31

Why did the author most likely write this passage?

A To persuade readers to visit Frederik Meijer Gardens

B To tell readers why they should study sculpture

C To entertain readers with a story about horses

D To inform readers about the development of a great statue

32

Why does the author begin the passage with a question?

A To ask the reader for assistance

B To tell the reader about Leonardo

C To capture the reader's attention

D To share an unusual riddle

33

The passage "A Horse from History" is an example of which type of literature?

A Essay

B Folktale

C Poetry

D Drama

34

Why was one of the two *Il Cavallo* statues given to Italy?

A Many Americans wanted to honor Italy's history and people.

B Most of the people who built the statues were Italian.

C Italy wanted a special gift from America.

D The statue would be displayed in Leonardo's hometown.

35

What is the most striking difference between Leonardo's first drawing and the finished statue?

A The drawing was lost for centuries, while the statue will never be lost.

B The drawing was as small as a stamp, while the statue is 24 feet tall.

C The drawing was very colorful, while the statue is only one color.

D The drawing was made carefully, while the statue was built carelessly.

GO ON ▶

36

Why does the author mention the stories of Leonardo weeping on his deathbed?

A To show that he felt he had not accomplished enough
B To show how much he cared for Ludovico Sforza
C To show that he had led an unhappy life
D To show how much his artwork meant to him

37

The author says that Leonardo benefited from his <u>well-rounded education</u>. What does this mean?

A His education was expensive.
B His education was brief.
C His education covered many topics.
D His education was limited to sculpting.

38

What was one difference between the "skin" of the statue and the "skeleton"?

A They were unlike Leonardo's drawing.
B The skeleton is stronger than the skin.
C The skin cost more than the skeleton.
D They were designed at different foundries.

39

Which is the best summary of this passage?

A A horse statue designed by Leonardo da Vinci is 24 feet tall.
B Horses are seen by many people to be symbols of peace and strength.
C A statue begun by Leonardo was finally built hundreds of years later.
D Clay models made by Leonardo were destroyed by French soldiers.

GO ON ▶

40

Which is most likely true of the horse experts who helped design the statue?

A They were not paid for their assistance.
B They explained horses' appearances.
C They were not supporters of Charles Dent.
D They were educated in metalwork.

41

Which statement from the passage shows that Leonardo loved to learn new things?

A "The city of Vinci had a long tradition of participation, and excellence, in the arts."
B "During this time, Leonardo began producing the amazing artwork that would earn him a place in history."
C "To fuel his creativity, Leonardo studied math, mechanics, architecture, anatomy, warfare, and nature."
D "Before he even turned 20, Leonardo was outdoing his master."

42

Based on the passage, what is a crossbow?

A A weapon
B A shop that specializes in statues
C A framework
D A tool for enlarging designs

43

Which of the following is the best summary of the third paragraph of the passage?

A Leonardo proved his skill in his youth.
B Leonardo dreamt of sculpting a giant horse.
C Del Verrochio stopped painting because of Leonardo.
D Del Verrochio was a master painter in Italy.

44

The author says that the statue is a noteworthy symbol of peace and strength. What does noteworthy mean?

A Striking
B Foreign
C Manufactured
D Bronzed

GO ON ▶

45 Why does the author include a "Quick Facts" box with the passage?

A To teach readers about how to make a statue

B To explain how to visit the statue

C To summarize information about the statue

D To tell readers the history of Leonardo

46 Where can an *Il Cavallo* statue be seen today?

A Vinci, Italy

B Michigan

C France

D Pennsylvania

GO ON ▶

47

If you were in charge of this project, would you give one of the two *Il Cavallo* statues as a gift to Italy? Use information from the passage to explain your answer.

Now read this passage and answer the questions that follow.

Center City Science Adventure

1   Have you ever wondered about the journey of a red blood cell as it gathers oxygen from the lungs and distributes it to other parts of your body? Have you ever thought about how thunderstorms form or how the nitrogen cycle works? If so, then Center City Science Adventure is the perfect place for you to experience science up close and personal.

2   Since 1997, Center City Science Adventure has established a reputation as an entertaining, educational expedition through the world of science. We pride ourselves on our massive, state-of-the-art replicas of human organ systems, our guided tours to the "center of the Earth," and our magnificent Milky Way Galaxy. Join us today and experience the wonder and exhilaration of our bodies, our minds, and our universe!

Center City Science Adventure
727 Wright Street
Center City
(555) SCI-ENCE

Take Exit 21A off Interstate 74W. Turn left at the Stop sign and follow Wright St. to Main Ave.

CHECK OUT OUR AMAZING EXHIBITS!

THE HUMAN BODY Tours:	SOLAR SYSTEM Tours:	EARTH SCIENCE Tours:
Circulation	The Nine Planets	Under the Sea
Respiration	The Moon	Earth's Cycles
Digestion	The Sun	Greenhouse Effect
Muscles and Bones	Comets and Asteroids	Weather Phenomenon
Ears and Eyes	Stars	Center of the Earth

3   Reserve your place on one of our daily excursions through the wonderful world of science. Parties of eight or more, please call to register at least two weeks in advance. **See our special rates for school field trips below.**

CENTER CITY SCIENCE ADVENTURE PRICE GUIDE

3-tour package	$15.00/person
6-tour package	$25.00/person
9-tour package	$35.00/person
2-day pass (all tours)	$50.00/person
Field trip special (5 tours)	**$9.00/child; $12.00/teacher or chaperone**

GO ON ▶

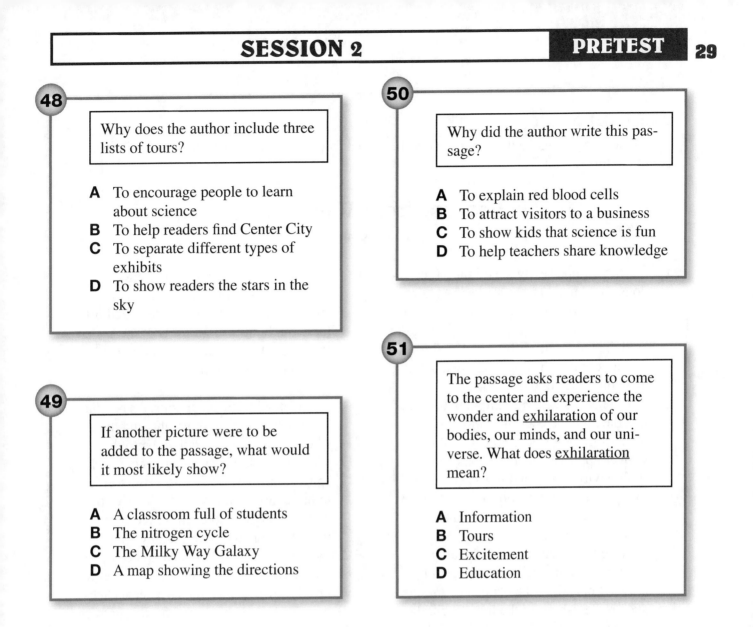

48 Why does the author include three lists of tours?

A To encourage people to learn about science
B To help readers find Center City
C To separate different types of exhibits
D To show readers the stars in the sky

50 Why did the author write this passage?

A To explain red blood cells
B To attract visitors to a business
C To show kids that science is fun
D To help teachers share knowledge

49 If another picture were to be added to the passage, what would it most likely show?

A A classroom full of students
B The nitrogen cycle
C The Milky Way Galaxy
D A map showing the directions

51 The passage asks readers to come to the center and experience the wonder and <u>exhilaration</u> of our bodies, our minds, and our universe. What does <u>exhilaration</u> mean?

A Information
B Tours
C Excitement
D Education

STOP

Session 3

Now read this passage and answer the questions that follow. You will have forty-five minutes to complete this session.

Excerpt from White Fang

by Jack London

1   They camped early that night. Three dogs could not drag the sled so fast nor for so long hours as could six, and they were showing unmistakable signs of playing out. And the men went early to bed, Bill first seeing to it that the dogs were tied out of gnawing-reach of one another.

2   But the wolves were growing bolder, and the men were aroused more than once from their sleep. So near did the wolves approach, that the dogs became frantic with terror, and it was necessary to replenish the fire from time to time in order to keep the adventurous marauders at safer distance.

3   "I've hearn sailors talk of sharks followin' a ship," Bill remarked, as he crawled back into the blankets after one such replenishing of the fire. "Well, them wolves is land sharks. They know their business better'n we do, an' they ain't a-holdin' our trail this way for their health. They're goin' to get us. They're sure goin' to get us, Henry."

4   "They've half got you a'ready, a-talkin' like that," Henry retorted sharply. "A man's half licked when he says he is. An' you're half eaten from the way you're goin' on about it."

5   "They've got away with better men than you an' me," Bill answered.

6   "Oh, shet up your croakin'. You make me all-fired tired."

7   Henry rolled over angrily on his side, but was surprised that Bill made no similar display of temper. This was not Bill's way, for he was easily angered by sharp words. Henry thought long over it before he went to sleep, and as his eyelids fluttered down and he dozed off, the thought in his mind was: "There's no mistakin' it, Bill's almighty blue. I'll have to cheer him up to-morrow."

    . . .

8   The day began auspiciously. They had lost no dogs during the night, and they swung out upon the trail and into the silence, the darkness, and the cold with spirits that were fairly light. Bill seemed to have forgotten his forebodings of the previous night, and even waxed facetious with the dogs when, at midday, they overturned the sled on a bad piece of trail.

9   It was an awkward mix-up. The sled was upside down and jammed between a tree-trunk and a huge rock, and they were forced to unharness the dogs in order to straighten out the tangle. The two men were bent over the sled and trying to right it, when Henry observed One Ear sidling away.

10   "Here, you, One Ear!" he cried, straightening up and turning around on the dog.

11   But One Ear broke into a run across the snow, his traces trailing behind him. And there, out in the snow of their back track, was the she-wolf waiting for him. As he neared her, he became suddenly cautious. He slowed down to an alert and mincing walk and then stopped. He regarded her carefully and dubiously, yet desirefully. She seemed to smile at him, showing her teeth in an ingratiating rather than a menacing way. She moved toward him

GO ON ▶

a few steps, playfully, and then halted. One Ear drew near to her, still alert and cautious, his tail and ears in the air, his head held high.

12   He tried to sniff noses with her, but she retreated playfully and coyly. Every advance on his part was accompanied by a corresponding retreat on her part. Step by step she was luring him away from the security of his human companionship. Once, as though a warning had in vague ways flitted through his intelligence, he turned his head and looked back at the overturned sled, at his team-mates, and at the two men who were calling to him.

13   But whatever idea was forming in his mind, was dissipated by the she-wolf, who advanced upon him, sniffed noses with him for a fleeting instant, and then resumed her coy retreat before his renewed advances.

14   In the meantime, Bill had bethought himself of the rifle. But it was jammed beneath the overturned sled, and by the time Henry had helped him to right the load, One Ear and the she-wolf were too close together and the distance too great to risk a shot.

15   Too late One Ear learned his mistake. Before they saw the cause, the two men saw him turn and start to run back toward them. Then, approaching at right angles to the trail and cutting off his retreat they saw a dozen wolves, lean and grey, bounding across the snow. On the instant, the she-wolf's coyness and playfulness disappeared. With a snarl she sprang upon One Ear. He thrust her off with his shoulder, and, his retreat cut off and still intent on regaining the sled, he altered his course in an attempt to circle around to it. More wolves were appearing every moment and joining in the chase. The she-

wolf was one leap behind One Ear and holding her own.

16   "Where are you goin'?" Henry suddenly demanded, laying his hand on his partner's arm.

17   Bill shook it off. "I won't stand it," he said. "They ain't a-goin' to get any more of our dogs if I can help it."

18   Gun in hand, he plunged into the underbrush that lined the side of the trail. His intention was apparent enough. Taking the sled as the centre of the circle that One Ear was making, Bill planned to tap that circle at a point in advance of the pursuit. With his rifle, in the broad daylight, it might be possible for him to awe the wolves and save the dog.

19   "Say, Bill!" Henry called after him. "Be careful! Don't take no chances!"

20   Henry sat down on the sled and watched. There was nothing else for him to do. Bill had already gone from sight; but now and again, appearing and disappearing amongst the underbrush and the scattered clumps of spruce, could be seen One Ear. Henry judged his case to be hopeless. The dog was thoroughly alive to its danger, but it was running on the outer circle while the wolf-pack was running on the inner and shorter circle. It was vain to think of One Ear so outdistancing his pursuers as to be able to cut across their circle in advance of them and to regain the sled.

21   The different lines were rapidly approaching a point. Somewhere out there in the snow, screened from his sight by trees and thickets, Henry knew that the wolf-pack, One Ear, and Bill were coming together. All too quickly, far more quickly than he had expected, it happened. He heard a shot, then two shots, in rapid succession, and he knew that Bill's ammunition was gone.

GO ON ▶

52

Which of the following words best describes Henry?

A Outraged
B Timid
C Rational
D Curious

53

Which is the best summary of this passage?

A Two friends are training for a dog sled race in the winter.
B Two men and a team of dogs encounter a pack of hungry wolves.
C A trained sled dog wants to escape into the wilderness.
D Dog sled racers accidentally overturn their sled on a harsh trail.

54

Why did One Ear sneak away from Bill and Henry?

A He caught the scent of meat and followed it.
B He was tired and wanted to take a nap.
C He started following another sled's trail and got lost.
D He was lured away by a female wolf.

55

What is Bill and Henry's main conflict in this passage?

A They have overturned their sled in the forest.
B Their dogs are too tired to pull their sled fast.
C They are being stalked by a pack of hungry wolves.
D Their dogs have pulled the sled off the main trail.

56

The passage says that Bill seemed to have forgotten his <u>forebodings</u> of the previous night. What does <u>forebodings</u> mean?

A Dreams
B Complaints
C Predictions
D Duties

57

Which word best describes the mood of this passage?

A Suspenseful
B Peaceful
C Depressing
D Frustrating

GO ON ▶

58

What is the theme of this passage?

A Friends are always there for each other in times of need.
B Don't judge a book by its cover.
C Fighting is not the way to solve problems.
D Man and nature are in constant struggle.

59

Why does Henry become concerned about Bill in the beginning of the passage?

A Bill seems as if he's becoming too weak and tired to continue.
B Bill doesn't respond to Henry's comments in his usual way.
C Henry is worried that the wolves will try to attack Bill in his sleep.
D Henry thinks that Bill needs to pay more attention to the dogs.

60

How does the she-wolf act toward One Ear at first?

A Viciously
B Excitedly
C Teasingly
D Carefully

61

What happens when One Ear tries to run from the she-wolf?

A He gets tangled up in his harness and falls.
B Several wolves appear and try to block his path.
C The sled overturns and gets stuck by a tree.
D He leads the wolves toward Bill and Henry.

62

Why does Bill take the rifle with him when he leaves Henry with the sled?

A He doesn't trust Henry to handle the rifle while he's gone.
B He thinks he can save One Ear by killing all of the wolves.
C He is going to fight the wolves away by hitting them with the gun.
D He is hoping that the sight and sound of the gun will scare the wolves.

GO ON ▶

63

Which quotation from the passage foreshadows that something bad will likely happen to Bill?

A "Bill had already gone from sight; but now and again, appearing and disappearing amongst the under-brush and the scattered clumps of spruce, could be seen One Ear."

B "He heard a shot, then two shots, in rapid succession, and he knew that Bill's ammunition was gone."

C "Henry rolled over angrily on his side, but was surprised that Bill made no similar display of temper."

D "This was not Bill's way, for he was easily angered by sharp words."

65

This excerpt from *White Fang* is an example of which type of literature?

A Essay
B Drama
C Fiction
D Autobiography

64

According to the passage, how are sharks and wolves similar?

A Like sharks that hunt for food, wolves are predators that feed on meat.

B Like sharks that follow sailors' ships, wolves are following Bill and Henry's sled.

C Like sharks that live in cold water, wolves enjoy living a cold environment.

D Like sharks that sometimes attack humans, wolves attack humans.

GO ON ▶

66 How can you tell that the wolves are going to attack Bill, Henry, and their dogs? Use information from the passage to support your answer.

Now read this passage and answer the questions that follow.

So You Want to Recycle?

1   You've probably seen recycling receptacles in many locations: the hallways at school, your favorite restaurant, a parent's or guardian's workplace, the mall, or the park. You try your best to deposit recyclable materials in the appropriate locations whenever possible, but sometimes, you wish you could do more. Recycling is one of the best--and simplest--ways to help the environment. Recycling saves time, energy, valuable resources, and money. So why not take the initiative and develop a recycling program in your own home?

Location, Location, Location

2   Developing a recycling center in your home is not as difficult as it sounds. It's simply a matter of choosing a good location, acquiring some storage containers, and letting your family in on your plan to save the environment.

3   The key to your recycling program success is to locate your recycling receptacles in an area that is easily accessible. No one in your family will want to trek through snow and rain to a shed located a hundred yards behind your house. Try finding an area in your house where you can stash a few recycling bins. Look for rooms that are centrally located, such as the kitchen or basement. You can also try stashing your recyclables in a cupboard or closet. If space is a problem, use smaller containers to hold your recyclables and make it your responsibility to move recyclable materials to a larger storage area in a garage or shed.

Gather It Up

4   Once you've chosen your location, choose storage containers of a suitable size and number for your recycling center. You can turn almost anything into recycling receptacles, such as paper grocery bags, old trash cans, cardboard boxes, crates, or old buckets. If you're not sure of the number of containers you need, check with local recycling centers to determine how recyclable materials should be sorted (for example, office paper, glass, plastic, cardboard, newspaper, and so on).

Recycle with Ease

5   Make recycling even easier for your family and friends by clearly labeling or posting pictures on each storage container so that everything gets sorted correctly. Now there's no excuse not to recycle!

Know Your Facts

6   According to the Illinois Recycling Association (IRA), it is estimated that recycling one ton of paper is the equivalent of saving seventeen trees, seven thousand gallons of water, and enough energy to power an average home for six months. The IRA also estimates that recycling in general saves enough energy each year to heat and light 400,000 Illinois homes. While this number is impressive, there is certainly room for improvement.

GO ON ▶

67

What is the purpose of the instructions in this passage?

A To persuade readers to learn more about recycling
B To instruct readers on creating a recycling center in their home
C To explain to readers how different materials are recycled
D To list for readers materials that can be recycled

69

Why did the author most likely write this passage?

A To provide readers with detailed information about recycling
B To inform readers of recycling rules in Illinois
C To illustrate how much recycling can help the environment
D To persuade people to practice recycling in their own homes

68

What advice does the author give about choosing a location for a recycling center?

A Pick a place that's easily accessible to all family members.
B Put recycling containers in the kitchen.
C It's better to use small containers than large ones.
D The best place for a recycling center is somewhere out of sight.

70

Why does the author include the "Know Your Facts" box with this passage?

A To explain how to get in touch with the Illinois Recycling Association
B To provide facts and figures about the benefits of recycling
C To indicate the proper way to sort recyclable items
D To discuss the process of recycling paper

STOP

ANSWER SHEETS

MARKING INSTRUCTIONS

Make heavy BLACK marks.
Erase cleanly.
Make no stray marks.

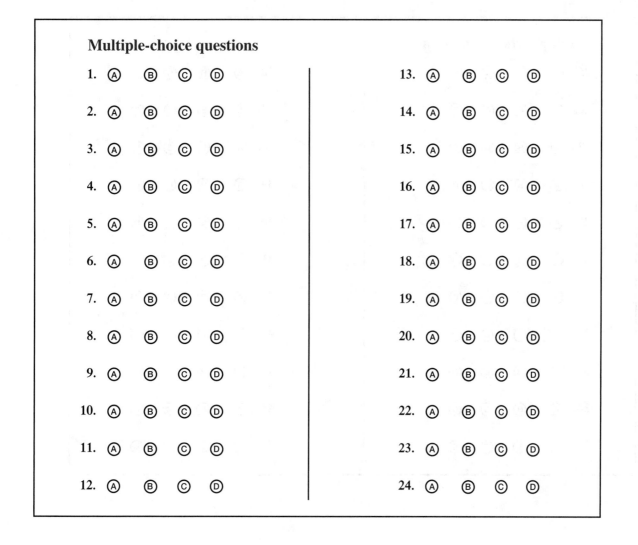

CORRECT MARK   INCORRECT MARK

Multiple-choice questions

1. Ⓐ Ⓑ © Ⓓ   13. Ⓐ Ⓑ © Ⓓ

2. Ⓐ Ⓑ © Ⓓ   14. Ⓐ Ⓑ © Ⓓ

3. Ⓐ Ⓑ © Ⓓ   15. Ⓐ Ⓑ © Ⓓ

4. Ⓐ Ⓑ © Ⓓ   16. Ⓐ Ⓑ © Ⓓ

5. Ⓐ Ⓑ © Ⓓ   17. Ⓐ Ⓑ © Ⓓ

6. Ⓐ Ⓑ © Ⓓ   18. Ⓐ Ⓑ © Ⓓ

7. Ⓐ Ⓑ © Ⓓ   19. Ⓐ Ⓑ © Ⓓ

8. Ⓐ Ⓑ © Ⓓ   20. Ⓐ Ⓑ © Ⓓ

9. Ⓐ Ⓑ © Ⓓ   21. Ⓐ Ⓑ © Ⓓ

10. Ⓐ Ⓑ © Ⓓ   22. Ⓐ Ⓑ © Ⓓ

11. Ⓐ Ⓑ © Ⓓ   23. Ⓐ Ⓑ © Ⓓ

12. Ⓐ Ⓑ © Ⓓ   24. Ⓐ Ⓑ © Ⓓ

Student Name_____

MARKING INSTRUCTIONS

Make heavy BLACK marks.
Erase cleanly.
Make no stray marks.

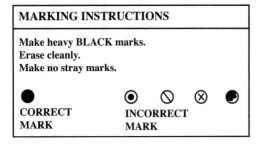

CORRECT
MARK

INCORRECT
MARK

Multiple-choice questions

25. Ⓐ	Ⓑ	Ⓒ	Ⓓ
26. Ⓐ	Ⓑ	Ⓒ	Ⓓ
27. Ⓐ	Ⓑ	Ⓒ	Ⓓ
28. Ⓐ	Ⓑ	Ⓒ	Ⓓ
29. Ⓐ	Ⓑ	Ⓒ	Ⓓ
30. Ⓐ	Ⓑ	Ⓒ	Ⓓ
31. Ⓐ	Ⓑ	Ⓒ	Ⓓ
32. Ⓐ	Ⓑ	Ⓒ	Ⓓ
33. Ⓐ	Ⓑ	Ⓒ	Ⓓ
34. Ⓐ	Ⓑ	Ⓒ	Ⓓ
35. Ⓐ	Ⓑ	Ⓒ	Ⓓ

36. Ⓐ	Ⓑ	Ⓒ	Ⓓ
37. Ⓐ	Ⓑ	Ⓒ	Ⓓ
38. Ⓐ	Ⓑ	Ⓒ	Ⓓ
39. Ⓐ	Ⓑ	Ⓒ	Ⓓ
40. Ⓐ	Ⓑ	Ⓒ	Ⓓ
41. Ⓐ	Ⓑ	Ⓒ	Ⓓ
42. Ⓐ	Ⓑ	Ⓒ	Ⓓ
43. Ⓐ	Ⓑ	Ⓒ	Ⓓ
44. Ⓐ	Ⓑ	Ⓒ	Ⓓ
45. Ⓐ	Ⓑ	Ⓒ	Ⓓ
46. Ⓐ	Ⓑ	Ⓒ	Ⓓ

Student Name_____

Write your final response for question 47 here.

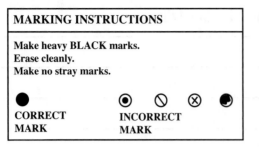

MARKING INSTRUCTIONS

Make heavy BLACK marks.
Erase cleanly.
Make no stray marks.

CORRECT
MARK

INCORRECT
MARK

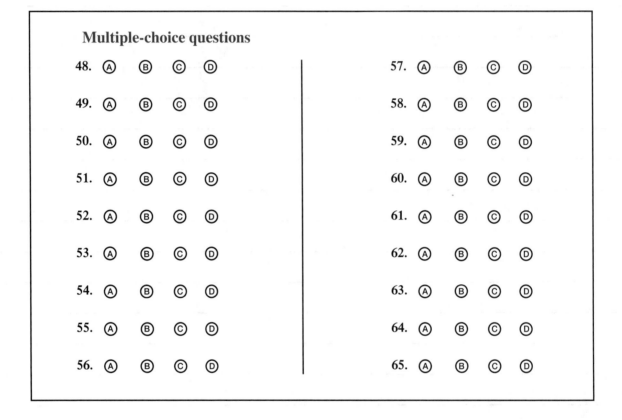

Multiple-choice questions

48.	Ⓐ	Ⓑ	Ⓒ	Ⓓ
49.	Ⓐ	Ⓑ	Ⓒ	Ⓓ
50.	Ⓐ	Ⓑ	Ⓒ	Ⓓ
51.	Ⓐ	Ⓑ	Ⓒ	Ⓓ
52.	Ⓐ	Ⓑ	Ⓒ	Ⓓ
53.	Ⓐ	Ⓑ	Ⓒ	Ⓓ
54.	Ⓐ	Ⓑ	Ⓒ	Ⓓ
55.	Ⓐ	Ⓑ	Ⓒ	Ⓓ
56.	Ⓐ	Ⓑ	Ⓒ	Ⓓ

57.	Ⓐ	Ⓑ	Ⓒ	Ⓓ
58.	Ⓐ	Ⓑ	Ⓒ	Ⓓ
59.	Ⓐ	Ⓑ	Ⓒ	Ⓓ
60.	Ⓐ	Ⓑ	Ⓒ	Ⓓ
61.	Ⓐ	Ⓑ	Ⓒ	Ⓓ
62.	Ⓐ	Ⓑ	Ⓒ	Ⓓ
63.	Ⓐ	Ⓑ	Ⓒ	Ⓓ
64.	Ⓐ	Ⓑ	Ⓒ	Ⓓ
65.	Ⓐ	Ⓑ	Ⓒ	Ⓓ

Student Name_____

Write your final response for question 66 here.

MARKING INSTRUCTIONS

Make heavy BLACK marks.
Erase cleanly.
Make no stray marks.

●   ◉   ⊘   ⊗   ◕

CORRECT   INCORRECT
MARK   MARK

Multiple-choice questions

67.   Ⓐ   Ⓑ   Ⓒ   Ⓓ   69.   Ⓐ   Ⓑ   Ⓒ   Ⓓ

68.   Ⓐ   Ⓑ   Ⓒ   Ⓓ   70.   Ⓐ   Ⓑ   Ⓒ   Ⓓ

Student Name_____

ANSWER KEY

Answer Key
Session 1

1   **D**   **1.8.24**   **RC**
The author discusses Adams' life and describes the events that led him to pursue a career in photography. Answer choice D is correct.

2   **B**   **1.8.03**   **V**
Adams was focused on a career in music until he published two books of photography. Afterward, he decided that he should focus on a career in photography. Answer choice B is the best answer.

3   **C**   **1.8.19**   **RC**
The author mentions that people still enjoy Adams' photographs even after his death. Adams dedicated a large portion of his life to capturing the beauty of Yosemite Valley and sharing it with others. The land was named after Adams to honor his dedication to and love for the Yosemite Valley. Answer choice C is the best answer.

4   **C**   **1.8.16**   **RC**
The paragraph explains how Adams' interest in photography led him to become interested in nature conservation as well. While the other answers may also be true, they are not stated in the passage and do not describe the main idea of the second paragraph.

5   **B**   **2.8.06**   **LET**
The article states that Adams admired Paul Strand's work and the unconventional methods that Strand used in his photography. The author also explains that Adams began to experiment with Strand's photographic techniques. While it is impossible to know exactly how Adams felt when he met Paul Strand, you can conclude that he most likely felt inspired by the photographer's work.

6   **B**   **2.8.11**   **LET**
While the mood of the story does appear to be serious, it does not suggest sadness. The speaker, who is creating the mood of the story, is not quiet or calm, nor does he create an environment that is exciting or adventurous. By insistently repeating his demands, the speaker is creating a tense environment that likely makes the other characters in the story uncomfortable. Answer choice B is the best answer.

7   **C**   **2.8.07**   **LET**
The speaker is trying to stress the importance of the children learning "facts." Answer choice C is the best answer choice.

8   **B**   **2.8.06**   **LET**
The speaker is not the students' teacher, since he tells someone to teach them facts in the beginning of the excerpt. He does not seem to be a parent, and we do not know if he is a friend of the schoolmaster. Answer choice B is the best answer.

9   **A**   **1.8.05**   **V**

The narrator says that the little vessels are ready to have facts poured into them. The speaker is stressing the importance of teaching facts to the students. You can conclude that the inclined plane of little vessels refers to the students in their seats.

10   **B**   **2.8.13**   **VLW**

The passage is part of a fictional story written by Charles Dickens. A biography is a story about a real person's life, and none of the characters in this passage are real people. An essay is written to inform readers on an author's personal point of view, and a myth is a story that attempts to explain the world view of a people. Answer choice B is the best answer choice.

11   **C**   **1.8.16**   **RC**

This paragraph of the passage describes how the scrolls were passed around until they were obtained by scholars who managed to identify them as ancient writings from people who once lived in Qumran. Though the other answer choices are mentioned, they do not describe the main idea of the paragraph.

12   **A**   **1.8.11**   **RS**

The passage tells you that archaeologists decided to excavate Qumran after finding scrolls, scroll fragments, pottery, cloth, and wood in Cave 1. Though the shepherds' discoveries most likely convinced scientists to excavate Cave 1, this is not the reason that they excavated the larger site of the ancient city of Qumran.

13   **A**   **2.8.11**   **LET**

The conclusion of the passage is mysterious because the author presents much unanswered information about the scrolls. There is no evidence to suggest that the author of the passage feels resentful, and the author does not present personal feelings of elation about the discoveries. If the author were indifferent, he may not have written the passage. Answer choice A is the correct answer.

14   **B**   **1.8.03**   **V**

When the archaeologists "dubbed" the cave "Qumran Cave 1," they gave it that name. If you were unable to determine this answer from the way the question was worded, you would be able to determine it by rereading the passage and looking at the way the word "dubbed" is used.

15   **C**   **2.8.13**   **VLW**

This passage is nonfiction. It is an article that describes real-life events. While some of the information in the article has not yet been proven, the article still describes the real-life discovery and excavation of the Dead Sea Scrolls. Answer choice C is the correct answer.

16   **A**   **2.8.06**   **LET**

After reading this passage, you can tell that the author's childhood was chaotic, but at the end of the passage the author expresses satisfaction with the societal change that took place. At times it was upsetting and gloomy, but this does not express the entirety of her childhood. At no point was her childhood boring. It may have been exciting and thrilling at times, but these terms do not express the hard times that the author experienced as a child.

17   C   1.8.21   RC
At the end of the passage, the author and her mother are allowed to sit at the front of the bus because the Supreme Court ruled that segregation on Montgomery public buses was illegal. Answer choice C is the correct answer.

18   C   2.8.13   VLW
The author of this passage is telling about her own life. This type of writing is called autobiography.

19   B   1.8.05   V
The author's pastor did not want the family to supply the city with money because the city was discriminating against them because of their race. While the word "furnish" can be used to illustrate decorating with furniture, in this context, it means supply. Answer choice B is correct.

20   C   1.8.24   RC
After reading the passage, you can tell that the author is mostly describing what it was like to grow up in a racially segregated city at an explosive time in American history. Though she may now love to sit at the front of the bus, this is not discussed in the passage.

21   D   1.8.19   RC
In the fourth paragraph of the passage, the author states that after moving to Wyoming, Margaret and her husband Olaus started a crusade of letters to convince the nation's leaders to protect wilderness areas. Answer choice D is the best answer.

22   B   1.8.16   RC
Answer choice B summarizes the main points of paragraph six of the passage. The other answer choices describe details from the paragraph, but do not provide the best summary of all points discussed in the paragraph. Answer choice B is the best answer.

23   A   1.8.11   RS
Margaret worked to have Alaskan lands designated as wildlife refuge areas so that the plants and animals on these lands would be protected by law. While the other answer choices may also describe Margaret's motivations, they are not stated in the passage.

24   B   1.8.05   V
Though the word "pioneer" can be used to describe a settler of a territory, in this context it means a person who helps open up a new line of thought or activity.

Margaret was one of the earliest figures to become vocal about her passion for protecting valuable wilderness areas, and to fight to have these areas protected. This is what President Bill Clinton meant when he referred to her as a pioneer. Answer choice B is correct.

25   D   2.8.06   LET

Though Margaret may have been all of the things described in these answer choices, without having known her and based solely on the information in this passage, we can only conclude that she was selfless and dedicated. She spent her whole life fighting to protect the environment so that everyone would be able to continue to enjoy it.

26   B   2.8.11   LET

The speaker's inability to pinpoint the origin of the looking-glass man makes him seem a bit uncertain. There is nothing in the poem to suggest that the speaker is weary or relieved, and the poem certainly does not suggest anger in any way. Answer choice B is the best answer.

27   D   1.8.19   RC

The speaker saw a man in a "looking-glass," which is a term used to describe a mirror. Even if you do not know the meaning of "looking-glass," you can still conclude that the speaker is looking in a mirror based on the idea that the man in the looking-glass does everything that the speaker does, and because the looking-glass man will always be with the speaker.

28   A   2.8.06   LET

The man in the looking-glass is a faithful companion because he will always be with the speaker. Though the speaker calls the man a "dreamer" and a "soldier," which might lead you to choose answer choices C or D, answer choice A is the best answer.

29   B   2.8.06   LET

The speaker most likely feels comforted, because he knows that the man in the looking-glass will always go with him, and that this is the only thing he cannot and will not lose. He does not seem unnerved, scared, or confused at the end of the poem. Answer choice B is the best answer.

30   B   1.8.24   RC

While you may think that the poet wrote the poem to inform readers about a strange character he encountered, you should always read all answer choices before making a final decision. The purpose of a poem or other piece of fiction is usually to entertain. The poet wrote this poem to entertain readers with an interesting expression of an ordinary idea. The ordinary idea or everyday occurrence here is an encounter with oneself in a mirror.

Session 2

31 D 1.8.24 RC
This passage is all about the development of a giant horse statue. The author's purpose is to inform readers about the statue.

32 C 1.8.24 RC
The author asks a riddle-like question at the beginning of the passage in order to capture the reader's interest so that he or she will keep reading in order to learn the answer to the question.

33 A 2.8.13 VLW
This passage contains factual information and no fictional elements. It can be best classified as an essay. Answer choice A is the best answer.

34 A 1.8.11 RS
The passage explains that one statue was given to Italy to honor Italy's people and history. Answer choice A is correct.

35 B 1.8.12 RS
If you were to compare the drawing of the statue design to the statue itself, the most striking difference is in size. The original drawing was the size of a postage stamp, while the statue stands over twenty-four feet tall.

36 D 1.8.24 RC
The author uses the story of Leonardo weeping to show how dedicated the artist was to his statue. Until he died, he was sorry he never finished it. Answer choice D is correct.

37 C 1.8.01 V
A well-rounded education is an education, like Leonardo's, that covers many topics. You can tell this by reading the passage. The passage states that Leonardo studied math, mechanics, architecture, anatomy, warfare, and nature. Answer choice C is best.

38 B 1.8.12 RS
If the skin and the skeleton of the statue were compared, the skeleton would prove to be stronger than the thin, bronze skin.

39 C 1.8.16 RC
The summary in answer choice C contains a brief description of the major points in this passage. The other answer choices describe details from the passage. Answer choice C is the best answer.

40 **B** **1.8.14** **RC**
The passage says that many experts were involved in the design of the horse statue. Horse experts would likely have been able to contribute the most information on the topic of horses' appearances. They were not, however, well-educated in metalwork.

41 **C** **1.8.19** **RC**
The answer choices all contain ideas from the passage, but only answer choice C deals with the topics that Leonardo studied. Answer choice C is best.

42 **A** **1.8.19** **RC**
In the passage, it says French soldiers fired crossbows at the clay model. You can safely conclude from that information that a crossbow is a weapon.

43 **A** **1.8.16** **RC**
All of the answer choices involve information from the passage, but only answer choice A summarizes the most important information in this paragraph.

44 **A** **1.8.03** **V**
This question asks the meaning of a word. Read the context of the word carefully and think about what you've learned about the horse. Answer choice A proves best.

45 **C** **1.8.25** **RC**
The Quick Facts box, included at the end of this passage, summarizes a lot of information about the topic of the passage.

46 **B** **1.8.21** **RC**
The passage tells you that one of the two Il Cavallo statues can be found today in Grand Rapids, Michigan.

47 **Extended Response** **1.8.19** **RC**
Sample answer: If I were in charge of the project to build a horse statue based on Leonardo da Vinci's designs, I would also want to give a copy of the statue to Italy. The main reason is that the idea for the statue came from Leonardo, an Italian. Since he never got the opportunity to make this statue, it seems fitting that his home country should be able to enjoy the version I made. Also, Il Cavallo is known as a symbol of peace. Everyone should share peace. Giving a symbol of peace to Italy is a wonderful gesture. It also thanks Italy for the many contributions it has made to the world.

48 **C** **1.8.25** **RS**
The three lists of tours in this passage are intended to separate the many kinds of tours into three main categories: Human Body, Solar System, and Earth Science.

49 **D** **1.8.23** **RC**
Considering the passage is meant to attract people to a special place, a map showing directions would likely be most useful.

50   **B**   **1.8.24**   **RC**
The author wants people to visit the Center City Science Adventure. Answer choice B is correct.

51   **C**   **1.8.03**   **V**
The author of the passage wants readers to get excited about the science center. Answer choice C is the correct answer.

Session 3

52   **C**   **2.8.06**   **LET**
Henry gets a little angry at Bill in the beginning of the passage, but he doesn't seem outraged. He is not timid because he's willing to stand up to Bill. By far the most curious character in the passage is One Ear. The word that best describes Henry is rational. Unlike Bill, who goes charging into the woods after the wolves, Henry calmly waits by the sled to see what will happen.

53   **B**   **1.8.16**   **RC**
The passage never mentions that Bill and Henry are in a race, which eliminates choices A and D. While One Ear gets distracted by the she-wolf, he doesn't want to escape into the wild. The correct answer is B. Bill, Henry, and their dogs are being pursued by a pack of wolves.

54   **D**   **1.8.18**   **RC**
One Ear was distracted by the she-wolf. She was acting playful and led him away from the safety of his owners.

55   **C**   **2.8.01**   **LET**
The passage never mentions the dogs pulling the sled off the main trail, so answer choice D is incorrect. Choices A, B, and C are all conflicts in the story. However, the main conflict is that Bill and Henry are being followed by a pack of wolves that keeps attacking their dogs.

56   **C**   **1.8.03**   **V**
On the previous night, Bill was concerned about the wolves following them and kept predicting that something bad was going to happen to them. When the author says that Bill forgot his forebodings, he means that Bill seemed to forget about his predictions.

57   **A**   **2.8.11**   **LET**
The mood of this story is certainly not peaceful. Bill and Henry are being followed by a pack of wolves that keeps attacking their dogs. While it may seem depressing or frustrating in some parts, the threat of the wolves attacking and the cliffhanger ending make the mood in the story suspenseful.

58 **D** **2.8.03** **LET**
This story illustrates the struggle between man and nature. Man is represented by Bill and Henry. Nature is represented by the wolves in the wilderness.

59 **B** **1.8.19** **RC**
The story says that Bill usually gets angered by sharp words, but he doesn't respond to Henry's comment. This makes Henry think that Bill is gloomy or depressed.

60 **C** **2.8.06** **LET**
At first, the she-wolf teases One Ear and pretends to play with him because she's trying to lead him away from Bill's and Henry's protection. Only later does she act viciously toward One Ear.

61 **B** **1.8.18** **RC**
When One Ear turns to run, a dozen wolves run across his path, trying to prevent him from reaching the sled.

62 **D** **1.8.14** **RC**
The story says, "With his rifle, in the broad daylight, it might be possible for him to awe the wolves and save the dog." Bill thinks that shooting the gun will distract the wolves from chasing One Ear. Answer choice D is the best answer.

63 **B** **2.8.11** **LET**
Choices A, C, and D do not foreshadow that anything bad will happen to Bill. However, choice B shows that Bill has run out of ammunition while trying to fend off a pack of wolves. Without ammunition, it can be assumed that Bill is in trouble.

64 **B** **1.8.12** **RS**
While some of the answers may be true, only one is mentioned in the story. According to Bill, sharks sometimes follow sailors' ships. He believes the wolves are doing the same thing: tracking Bill and Henry's sled through the snow.

65 **C** **2.8.13** **VLW**
White Fang is a fictional story written by Jack London. Essays and autobiographies are nonfiction and drama refers to works that are performed on the stage (plays).

66 **Extended-response** **1.8.19** **RC**
Sample answer: According to the story, the wolves are getting bolder and are moving closer and closer to Bill and Henry's camp. Bill makes the remark that he thinks the wolves are following them, just like sharks that follow sailors' ships. Comparing the wolves to sharks makes them seem even more vicious. Later, One Ear gets lured away by a female wolf. She pretends to want to play, and then, when One Ear gets too close, she turns on him and begins to chase him. All of these clues lead up to the final scene, when a dozen other wolves attack and try to block One Ear's path, and Bill heads into the woods with a rifle to try and scare them away.

67 **B** **1.8.23** **RC**

While the passage does persuade readers to recycle, the main goal of the instructions is to teach readers how to set up a recycling area in their home.

68 **A** **1.8.23** **RC**

The author says that you could place containers in the kitchen, but doesn't say that you have to. Also, the author only recommends using small containers, if you don't have room for large ones. The author never mentions placing the recycling center out of sight.

69 **D** **1.8.24** **RC**

While part of the passage does illustrate how much recycling can help the environment, the author's main purpose is to persuade people to practice recycling in their own home by providing instructions for creating a quick and easy recycling center.

70 **B** **1.8.24** **RC**

The box includes some impressive facts and figures about recycling. The author most likely included it to show how beneficial recycling can be for the environment.

Reading

Lesson 1: Vocabulary

Standard 1A: Vocabulary Development

(1.8.01)   **Determine the meaning of an unknown word or content-area vocabulary using knowledge of prefixes, suffixes, and word roots.**

(1.8.02)   **Use etymologies to determine the meanings of words.**

(1.8.03)   **Determine the meaning of an unknown word using word, sentence, and cross-sentence clues.**

(1.8.04)   **Determine the connotation of a word using word, sentence, and cross-sentence clues.**

(1.8.05)   **Determine the meaning of a word in context when the word has multiple meanings.**

Vocabulary Questions

To answer vocabulary questions on the ISAT, you may have to use your knowledge of prefixes, suffixes, and word roots to figure out the meaning of the word. For example, you might not know the meaning of the word *imperceptible*, but you might know that the prefix *im-* means not, so you can figure out that the word means "not perceptible." You might have to determine the meaning of the rest of the word from its **context,** meaning how the word is used in the passage. You can often find clues to a word's meaning from looking at the sentence the word is in and surrounding sentences.

Vocabulary questions on the ISAT might also ask you to explain the meaning of a phrase containing **figurative language,** language that is not meant to be taken literally. For example, if one character tells another to "zip it up," the first character wants the second to be quiet.

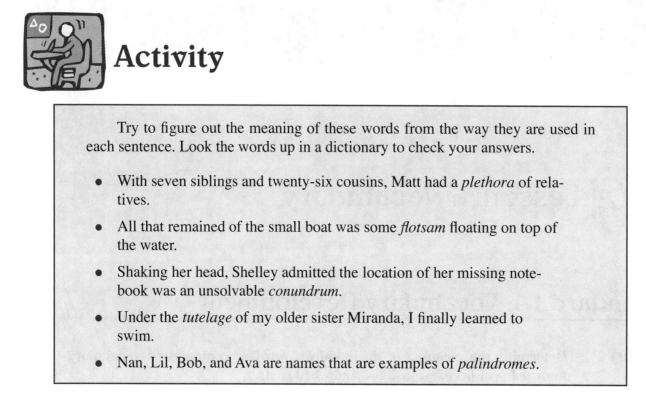

Activity

Try to figure out the meaning of these words from the way they are used in each sentence. Look the words up in a dictionary to check your answers.

- With seven siblings and twenty-six cousins, Matt had a *plethora* of relatives.

- All that remained of the small boat was some *flotsam* floating on top of the water.

- Shaking her head, Shelley admitted the location of her missing notebook was an unsolvable *conundrum*.

- Under the *tutelage* of my older sister Miranda, I finally learned to swim.

- Nan, Lil, Bob, and Ava are names that are examples of *palindromes*.

Passage 1

Now read this passage and answer the questions that follow.

The Reverse of the Curse

Take Me Out to the Ballgame

As they do every October, baseball fans across the country anxiously awaited the start of the World Series in 1919. That fall, the Chicago White Sox were set to play against the Cincinnati Reds. Baseball had recently enjoyed a surge in popularity due to the end of World War I, and the teams would play a best-of-nine-game series in front of hundreds of fans. Though many expected a fair fight for the championship, what happened that year changed baseball forever, and seemed to seal the fate of the White Sox for years to come.

The Scandal

That season, the White Sox were the best team in baseball, favored to win the World Series against the Reds. However, before the first pitch was thrown, events were set into motion that would ensure a Reds victory that year. Several Chicago players, including first baseman Chick Gandil and the famous "Shoeless" Joe Jackson, met with professional gamblers to fix the games. In all, eight of the White Sox players were involved in a plan to throw the World Series. By doing this, each player would receive a specific sum of money from the gamblers. By already knowing the outcome, the gamblers were sure to win any bet they made. Of course, rigging a professional sporting event like the World Series is a crime, and all of the players would later pay dearly for their involvement.

The 1919 Series

The White Sox's performance during the series was noticeably poorer than the effort the team had put forth during the rest of the season. Several officials noticed this, but the series went on as planned. The White Sox ended up losing the series, winning just three of the eight games that were actually played. The players involved in the scheme made plenty of errors. It was obvious to their teammates and many devoted fans that something was not right. Rumors began to spread that the team had lost on purpose. After the series' end, no immediate action against the players was taken, but that soon changed.

The Aftermath

In 1920, a grand jury was set up to investigate what had happened during the World Series the previous year. The players were questioned by law enforcement officials, and two of the White Sox eventually admitted that they had been involved in the conspiracy, or plot, to throw the series. The investigation led officials to create the role of Commissioner of Baseball, a position that would regulate players' actions and one that still exists today. The inaugural Commissioner was Federal

Judge Kenesaw Mountain Landis. Landis carefully reviewed the case against the White Sox players. Though all of them had been acquitted during the criminal trial because evidence against them went missing under suspicious circumstances, Landis decided to ban all eight players from the sport of baseball forever. The two players who had confessed later recanted their earlier statements, proclaiming their innocence, but neither would play professionally again.

The Curse

Following the 1919 World Series, the Chicago White Sox didn't make it to another championship until 1959, which they also lost. Fans didn't just see this as a long losing streak; they considered the team cursed by the players that ruined the White Sox's previous chance to win a series. This seemingly unending string of losses became known as the Curse of the Black Sox. The term "Black Sox" likely refers to the underhanded and dark conspiracy that surrounded the 1919 series, though some baseball experts debate the origin of the name. To Chicago fans and the rest of the sports world, it seemed that the misdeeds of a few players would plague the team forever. But, in 2005, the curse was miraculously lifted.

The Reverse

In October of 2005, the White Sox again made it to the World Series, where they faced the Houston Astros. The two teams played a best-of-seven-game series; Chicago had the home field advantage for the first game. Over 41,000 White Sox fans packed the stands and watched their team take an early lead in the series by winning the first game, five runs to three. The White Sox went on to win the next three games, sweeping the Astros, four games to none. With their 2005 World Series victory, the first for the team in eighty-eight years, the Chicago White Sox not only became champions, they also lifted a curse that had followed the franchise for nearly a century!

 Questions

1 The passage says that eight of the White Sox players were involved in the plan to <u>throw</u> the World Series. What does this mean?

A They flung the World Series ball out of the stadium.
B They lost the World Series on purpose.
C They tossed the World Series to the other team.
D They propelled the World Series trophy.

 Tip

The word "throw" can be used in several different ways. Look at all of the choices and consider the way in which the word is used in the sentence, as well as what you've read in the passage. Then decide which of the choices best fits.

2 The passage says that the <u>inaugural</u> Commissioner was Federal Judge Kenesaw Mountain Landis. What does <u>inaugural</u> mean?

A First
B Meanest
C Best
D Highest

 Tip

If you don't already know the meaning of this word, go back to the passage and reread the part of the passage that contains this sentence. Look at the words and sentences that surround the word "inaugural." Then choose the best answer based on what you've learned from the passage.

3   The passage says that the two players who had confessed to the crime later <u>recanted</u> their testimonies, proclaiming their innocence. What does <u>recanted</u> mean?

   A   Told the truth
   B   Took back
   C   Snuck around
   D   Stated again

Tip

You can tell the meaning of this word just by looking at the sentence. Read the sentence again and think about what it is saying. What can it tell you about the meaning of the word "recanted"?

4   According to the passage, baseball saw a <u>surge</u> in popularity due to the end of World War I. What does <u>surge</u> mean?

   A   Excitement
   B   Power
   C   Pouring
   D   Increase

Tip

Look at how the word is used in the sentence and think about what you read in the beginning of passage. Can you spot any clues that might help you figure out the meaning of this word?

Now check your answers on the next page.

Passage 1: "The Reverse of the Curse"

 Answers

1. **B** By substituting the answer choices, you can see that the way "throw" is used in the sentence means that the players were trying to lose the game. The best choice is B.

2. **C** After reading the passage, you know that the position of Commissioner of Baseball was a newly created position at this time. While some may have thought that banning players from the sport of baseball was mean, this is not the best answer. From the information in the passage, you can tell that Landis was the first Commissioner. The best answer choice is C.

3. **B** The word comes from the Latin word "recantare" which literally means "to sing again." This means that a person is taking back what she or he once said, and now saying something else. If you don't already know this, you can use the clues in the sentence to guess the meaning of this word. The sentence says that the players who had originally confessed now claimed that they were innocent. Answer choice B is correct.

4. **D** According to the passage, after this "surge" in popularity, hundreds of fans watched the World Series. Based on this information, you can tell that a "surge" in popularity is an increase in popularity. Substituting the word "surge" with each answer choice can also help you choose the right answer to this question.

Passage 2

Now read this passage and answer the questions that follow.

Iroquois Dreams

Long before Europeans ventured into what is now the State of New York, native Indians from the Iroquois, Mohawk, Oneida, Onondaga, and Cayuga tribes formed the mighty Iroquois Nation. This group of Indians thrived due to its strong political organization, military power, and sense of unity. Though historians credit several factors for the Iroquois strength, the Iroquois themselves attribute much of their success to their ability to follow their dreams.

The Iroquois use their dreams as a guide to every part of their lives. They rely on their dreams to lead them in everything from marriage to hunting to battle. In fact, if a tribal member dreamed of failure in battle, the tribe would retreat or postpone their attempt. Throughout their history, dreams were very important to the Iroquois way of life. The Iroquois listen carefully to their dreams and follow their dreams with precision. In fact, the Iroquois feel that to disobey even one dream could bring great misfortune.

There are many examples of how the Iroquois viewed their future through their dreams. Because they wanted to be sure of what their dreams meant, they used the skills of other tribal members who were known as dream interpreters. One historic example is of a mother who dreamed that her unborn son would become a great peacemaker. Her son became a famous Iroquois chief named Ely Parker.

Before his birth, Parker's mother dreamed of seeing a broken rainbow stretching from a white man's home in Buffalo to her reservation in Indian Falls. Disturbed by the dream and confused by its possible meaning, she visited a dream interpreter. The dream interpreter told her that her son would grow up to be a great peacemaker. The interpreter went on to explain that her son would become famous among both the Iroquois and the white man. As it turns out, Parker grew to become a leader for the Union in the Civil War. In the end, he played a significant role in writing the terms of surrender for the Civil War. Parker did indeed become a learned man who was admired by both the white man and the Iroquois.

It's easy to see why the Iroquois put so much effort into accurately understanding their dreams. They felt that dreams could cure disease and lead them to the secret longings of their souls. They also

felt that to disobey or ignore dreams would bring about illness and disaster not only for themselves but for fellow tribal members. The Iroquois would often gather to share their dreams and discuss their interpretations. They also gathered to reenact their dreams, acting out their dreams with other members of the tribe.

These community get-togethers often involved the False Face Society, which consisted of chosen Iroquois who wore carved masks and performed dances. There were several major ceremonies throughout the year where the False Face Society would lead dream interpretations. One of the biggest ceremonies was called the Midwinter Dream Festival, which ends the old year and brings in the new year. The festival centers on thanksgiving for the past and hope for the future. The lessons and healing from past dreams are remembered in song and dance. The mothers and grandmothers of the tribe also take part in a ritual called dreamsharing. They gather to share dreams they felt were helpful and dreams that they felt were confusing and needed further interpretation.

In the Ceremony of the Great Riddle, the Iroquois told their dreams to experts in dream guessing. These experts gave the dreamers hints as to what the dreams really meant. If the dreamer felt that the dream expert was helpful in finding the true meaning of the dream, the dreamer gave a token gift to the interpreter.

The Iroquois also used handmade dreamcatchers to catch their dreams and to protect them from nightmares. Dreamcatchers have become popular decorations for many people today, but the Iroquois as well as other American Indians relied on them to catch their dreams, both good and bad. The beads that were woven into the dreamcatcher were meant to guide good dreams through the center hole of the dreamcatcher web, while the bad dreams would get caught in the web. The good dreams would go through the hole and follow the feathers off the dreamcatcher and into another night's dream.

 **Questions**

1   The article says that the Iroquois <u>attribute</u> much of their success to their ability to follow their dreams. What does <u>attribute</u> mean?

   A   Think
   B   Attach
   C   Credit
   D   Consider

 Tip

Substitute each of the answer choices in the sentence. Choose the answer choice that best fits.

2 The article says that Ely Parker played a role in writing the terms of surrender for the Civil War and was a <u>learned man</u> who was admired by all. What does this mean?

    A   Ely Parker knew a great deal.

    B   Ely Parker was taught by others.

    C   Ely Parker needed to know more.

    D   Ely Parker attended school for many years.

 Tip

Think about what Ely Parker did. Did he need to know a lot to do this? Do you think he was able to attend school?

3 The article says that the Iroquois gathered to <u>reenact</u> their dreams by acting them out. What does <u>reenact</u> mean?

    A   To act again

    B   To try to remember

    C   To think about

    D   To tell others about

 Tip

Read this part of the passage again and consider each answer choice before choosing the correct one.

Check your answers with those on the next page. Be sure to read the explanation after each answer.

Passage 2: "Iroquois Dreams"

 **Answers**

1. C If you substitute each answer choice, you can see that "credit" is the best answer. While substituting the answer choices does not always help you find the right answer, it can often clue you in to the best answer choice.

2. A When the author says that Ely Parker was a learned man, he or she means that Parker knew a great deal. Parker would not have been able to attend school, but he would have been able to learn on his own.

3. A The prefix *re-* means "again." When the Iroquois reenacted their dreams, they acted them out so they could see them again. Answer choice A is the best answer.

Passage 3

Now read this passage and answer the questions that follow.

Excerpt from *Incidents in the Life of a Slave Girl*
by Harriet Jacobs

Much as I despise and detest the class of slave-traders, whom I regard as the vilest wretches on earth, I must do this man the justice to say that he seemed to have some feeling. He took a fancy to William in the jail, and wanted to buy him. When he heard the story of my children, he was willing to aid them in getting out of Dr. Flint's power, even without charging the customary fee.

My uncle procured a wagon and carried William and the children back to town. Great was the joy in my grandmother's house! The curtains were closed, and the candles lighted. The happy grandmother cuddled the little ones to her bosom. They hugged her, and kissed her, and clapped their hands, and shouted. She knelt down and poured forth one of her heartfelt prayers of thanksgiving to God. The father was present for a while; and though such a "parental relation" as existed between him and my children takes slight hold of the hearts or consciences of slaveholders, it must be that he experienced some moments of pure joy in witnessing the happiness he had imparted.

I had no share in the rejoicings of that evening.

The events of the day had not come to my knowledge. And now I will tell you something that happened to me; though you will, perhaps, think it illustrates the superstition of slaves. I sat in my usual place on the floor near the window, where I could hear much that was said in the street without being seen. The family had retired for the night, and all was still. I sat there thinking of my children, when I heard a low strain of music. A band of serenaders were under the window, playing "Home, sweet home." I listened till the sounds did not seem like music, but like the moaning of children. It seemed as if my heart would burst. I rose from my sitting posture, and knelt. A streak of moonlight was on the floor before me, and in the midst of it appeared the forms of my two children. They vanished; but I had seen them distinctly. Some will call it a dream, others a vision. I know not how to account for it, but it made a strong impression on my mind, and I felt certain something had happened to my little ones. . . .

At dawn, Betty was up and off to the kitchen. The hours passed on, and the vision of the night kept constantly recurring to my thoughts. After a while I heard the voices of two women in the entry. In one of them I recognized the housemaid. The other said to her, "Did you know Linda Brent's children was sold to the speculator[1] yesterday. They say ole massa Flint was mighty glad to see 'em drove out of town; but they say they've come back again. I 'spect it's all their daddy's doings. They say he's bought William too. Lor! how it will take hold of ole massa Flint! I'm going roun' to aunt Marthy's to see 'bout it."

I bit my lips till the blood came to keep from crying out. Were my children with their grandmother, or had the speculator carried them off? The suspense was dreadful. Would Betty never come, and tell me the truth about it? At last she came, and I eagerly repeated what I had overheard. Her face was one broad, bright smile....

---

[1]**speculator:** a slave trader

… Great surprise was expressed when it was known that my children had returned to their grandmother's. The news spread through the town, and many a kind word was bestowed on the little ones.

Dr. Flint went to my grandmother's to ascertain who was the owner of my children, and she informed him. "I expected as much," said he. "I am glad to hear it. I have had news from Linda lately, and I shall soon have her. You need never expect to see her free. She shall be my slave as long as I live, and when I am dead she shall be the slave of my children. If I ever find out that you or Phillip had any thing to do with her running off I'll kill him. And if I meet William in the street, and he presumes to look at me, I'll flog him within an inch of his life. Keep those brats out of my sight!"

As he turned to leave, my grandmother said something to remind him of his own doings. He looked back upon her, as if he would have been glad to strike her to the ground.

I had my season of joy and thanksgiving. It was the first time since my childhood that I had experienced any real happiness. I heard of the old doctor's threats, but they no longer had the same power to trouble me. The darkest cloud that hung over my life had rolled away. Whatever slavery might do to me, it could not shackle my children. If I fell a sacrifice, my little ones were saved. It was well for me that my simple heart believed all that had been promised for their welfare. It is always better to trust than to doubt.

A small shed had been added to my grandmother's house years ago. Some boards were laid across the joists at the top, and between these boards and the roof was a very small garret, never occupied by anything but rats and mice. It was a pent roof, covered with nothing but shingles, according to the southern custom for such buildings. The garret was only nine feet long and seven wide. The highest part was three feet high, and sloped down abruptly to the loose board floor. There was no admission for either light or air. My uncle Phillip, who was a carpenter, had very skillfully made a concealed trap-door, which communicated with the storeroom. He had been doing this while I was waiting in the swamp. The storeroom opened upon a piazza. To this hole I was conveyed as soon as I entered the house. The air was stifling; the darkness total. A bed had been spread on the floor. I could sleep quite comfortably on one side; but the slope was so sudden that I could not turn on the other without hitting the roof. The rats and mice ran over my bed; but I was weary, and I slept such sleep as the wretched may, when a tempest has passed over them.

Morning came. I knew it only by the noises I heard; for in my small den day and night were all the same. I suffered for air even more than for light. But I was not comfortless. I heard the voices of my children. There was joy and there was sadness in the sound. It made my tears flow. How I longed to speak to them! I was eager to look on their faces; but there was no hole, no crack, through which I could peep. This continued darkness was oppressive. It seemed horrible to sit or lie in a cramped position day after day, without one gleam of light. Yet I would have chosen this, rather than my lot as a slave, though white people considered it an easy one; and it was so compared with the fate of others. I was never cruelly overworked; I was never lacerated with the whip from head to foot; I was never so beaten and bruised that I could not turn from one side to the other; I never had my heel-strings cut to prevent my running away; I was never chained to a log and forced to drag it about, while I toiled in the fields from morning till night; I was never branded with hot iron, or torn by bloodhounds. On the contrary, I had always been kindly treated, and tenderly cared for, until I came into the hands of Dr. Flint. I had never wished for freedom until then. But though my life in slavery was comparatively devoid of hardships, God pity the woman who is compelled to lead such a life!

My food was passed up to me through the trap-door my uncle had contrived; and my grandmother, my uncle Phillip, and aunt Nancy would seize such opportunities as they could, to mount up there and chat with me at the opening. But of course this was not safe in the daytime. It must all be done in darkness. It was impossible for me to move in an erect position, but I crawled about my den for exercise. One day I hit my head against something, and found it was a gimlet.[2] My uncle had left it sticking there when he made the trap-door. I was as rejoiced as Robinson Crusoe could have been at finding such a treasure. It put a lucky thought into my head. I said to myself, "Now I will have some light. Now I will see my children." I did not dare to begin my work during the daytime, for fear of attracting attention. But I grouped round; and having found the side next the street, where I could frequently see my children, I stuck the gimlet in and waited for the evening. I bored three rows of holes, one above another; then I bored out the interstices between. I thus succeeded in making one hold about an inch long and an inch broad. I sat by it till late into the night, to enjoy the little whiff of air that floated in. In the morning I watched for my children. The first person I saw in the street was Dr. Flint. I had a shuddering, superstitious feeling that it was a bad omen. Several familiar faces passed by. At last I heard the merry laugh of children, and presently two sweet little faces were looking up at me, as though they knew I was there, and were conscious of the joy they imparted. How I longed to *tell* them I was there!

My condition was now a little improved. But for weeks I was tormented by hundreds of little red insects, fine as a needle's point, that pierced through my skin, and produced an intolerable burning. The good grandmother gave me herb teas and cooling medicines, and finally I got rid of them. The heat of my den was intense, for nothing but thin shingles protected me from the scorching summer's sun. But I had my consolations. Through my peeping-hole I could watch the children, and when they were near enough, I could hear their talk. . . . [Then] [a]utumn came, with a pleasant abatement of heat.

My eyes had become accustomed to the dim light, and by holding my book or work in a certain position near the aperture I contrived to read and sew. That was a great relief to the tedious monotony of my life. But when winter came, the cold penetrated through the thin shingle roof, and I was dreadfully chilled. The winters there are not so long, or so severe, as in northern latitudes; but the houses are not built to shelter from cold, and my little den was peculiarly comfortless. The kind grandmother brought me bed-clothes and warm drinks. Often I was obliged to lie in bed all day to keep comfortable; but with all my precautions, my shoulders and feet were frostbitten. O, those long, gloomy days, with no object for my eye to rest upon, and no thoughts to occupy my mind, except the dreary past and the uncertain future! I was thankful when there came a day sufficiently mild for me to wrap myself up and sit at the loophole to watch the passers by. Southerners have the habit of stopping and talking in the streets, and I heard many conversations not intended to meet my ears. I heard slave-hunters planning how to catch some poor fugitive. Several times I heard allusions to Dr. Flint, myself, and the history of my children, who, perhaps, were playing near the gate. . . . The opinion was often expressed that I was in the Free States. Very rarely did any one suggest that I might be in the vicinity. Had the least suspicion rested on my grandmother's house, it would have been burned to the ground.

But it was the last place they thought of. Yet there was no place, where slavery existed, that could have afforded me so good a place of concealment.

Dr. Flint and his family repeatedly tried to coax and bribe my children to tell something they had heard said about me. One day the doctor took them into a shop, and offered them some bright little silver pieces and gay handkerchiefs if they would tell where their mother was. Ellen shrank away from him, and would not speak; but Benny spoke up, and said, "Dr. Flint, I don't know where my mother is. I guess she's in New York; and when you go there again, I wish you'd ask her to come home, for I want to see her; but if you put her in jail, or tell her you'll cut her head off, I'll tell her to go right back."

---

[2] **gimlet:** a hand drill

 Questions

1　The narrator says that she lived in a <u>garret</u>, created by some boards that were laid across the joists at the top of the house. What does <u>garret</u> mean?

A　House
B　Attic
C　Bedroom
D　Garage

 Tip

The garret is near the top of the house. The narrator says the highest part was only three feet high and then sloped down abruptly. Where do you think the garret was?

2　In the story, the narrator says that when she knew her children were no longer slaves, "the <u>darkest cloud that hung over my life had rolled away</u>." What does this mean?

A　She was relieved.
B　She became angry.
C　She was finally able to see.
D　She was freed from slavery.

 Tip

If you're unsure of the meaning of this phrase, begin by eliminating answer choices that are obviously incorrect. Then consider how the narrator felt when she learned her children were free.

3   The story says that Dr. Flint went to the narrator's grandmother's to <u>ascertain</u> who owned her children. Which word means the same as <u>ascertain</u>?

A   Ask
B   Request
C   Determine
D   Prompt

  Tip

Dr. Flint is trying to find out who owns the narrator's children. Which answer choice is the best answer?

4   The narrator says that her life as a slave was relatively <u>devoid</u> of hardships. What does <u>devoid</u> mean?

A   Incomplete
B   Wanting
C   Without
D   Packed

 **Tip**

If you're not sure of the meaning of "devoid," reread the part of the story where the narrator discusses her life as a slave. How was her life different from other slaves?

Check your answers on the next page.

Passage 3: "Excerpt from *Incidents in the Life of a Slave Girl*"

 Answers

1. B   You can tell that the garret is the attic by reading the author's description of the garret in the passage. The fact that it is near the top of the house and that the walls slope down tells you that it is a room in the roof.

2. A   The dark cloud hanging over the narrator's life is the worry that she feels in knowing that her children are bound to slavery. When she knows they are free, she feels relief. Answer choice A is correct.

3. C   The narrator is hiding from Dr. Flint, the villain of the story. Knowing this, even though you might at first think that "ascertain" might mean "ask," you can guess that Dr. Flint will not expect to get a straight answer if he asks the grandmother a question about the children. Using context clues, you can guess that the meaning of "ascertain" is "determine."

4. C   In this part of the passage, the narrator says that she was always treated kindly and cared for until she came into the ownership of Dr. Flint. She was not branded or torn into by bloodhounds. The correct answer is C.

Passage 4

Now read this passage and answer the questions that follow.

The Birth of Golf

Hundreds of years ago, most people relied on the land in order to survive. They would spend many hours every day growing crops, gathering wood, and herding animals. Since they spent their days largely out-of-doors, they were of course surrounded by rocks and sticks. It seems only natural that, when they found a few minutes for recreation, they would create games using this makeshift equipment.

Many historians believe that as far back as the reign of Julius Caesar around 2,000 years ago people were playing a game that involved striking a round pebble or a ball with a tree branch. However, it wasn't until the Middle Ages that this sort of game became very popular. Around 1400, many countries throughout Europe had adopted variations of this simple pastime. The Dutch and Irish played it on the ice of their frozen lakes and canals. This game, called Shinty or Hurling, resembled modern-day hockey.

Other people of other nationalities played differently, but the most unique version of the game developed in eastern Scotland in the 1400s. Here, as legend has it, bored shepherds took up the club-and-ball pastime as many others before them had. However, the geographic characteristics of the Scottish coast—which included grassy tracks, sand dunes, and, most importantly, rabbit holes—made these shepherds' game very special. The shepherds not only hit the pebbles, but they practiced aiming and swinging in order to send the pebbles far out into the meadows and into the rabbit holes. Whoever could get the pebble into the rabbit hole with the least amount of swings was the winner. The Scottish shepherds called this pastime "gowf."

Once the idea of adding holes spread throughout Europe, most people modified the games they'd been playing. The game became more popular than ever. Soon, England had "goff," the Netherlands had "kolf," and France and Belgium had their own variations. Royalty and peasants alike wanted to participate in this new sport, which would evolve over generations into what we know today as golf.

The game made an impact immediately. It was immensely popular with the citizens of Scotland, who were so enthusiastic about the game that they devoted much of their time to it. They spent so much time playing sports like golf that they neglected their duty to King James II; specifically, they shrugged off their obligation to train for the military. The enraged king, seeing his military might suffering because of the people's obsession with sticks and pebbles, declared golf illegal in 1457!

Even a royal reproach was not enough to stop the Scottish people from enjoying their sport. They created golf courses, called links, along the sandy seashores of their nation. People flocked to these links day in and day out. The most popular link was named St. Andrews. At its beginning it was just a single small tract of land surrounded by bushes and heather shrubs; as more and more people visited it, it began to grow tremendously. The visiting golfers brought business to the surrounding cities, and suddenly there was a great call for golf clubs, balls, as well as caddies (golfers' assistants). The owners of St. Andrews worked over the next generations to expand their golf course, and today it is the largest golfing complex in Europe. At the time, however, golf was still illegal!

The outlook for the new sport brightened almost 50 years later, when King James IV decided the banned pastime was actually quite entertaining. Not only did he lift the ban, but his interest in the sport, like a celebrity endorsement today, made golf more popular than ever. King James himself began playing golf in 1502; in fact, some believe that he was the first person to officially purchase a full set of golf clubs. The royalty of England and Scotland began teaching foreign rulers how to golf.

The sport took a strong hold in France; however, the heart of golf remained in Scotland. The capitol of the country, Edinburgh, hosted the world's most famous golf course, called Leith. In 1744, the first golfers' organization, the Gentleman Golfers, formed at Leith. They originated the idea of golf tournaments, yearly competitions featuring impressive trophy prizes. Additionally, they devised a set of rules for the game that were widely accepted.

Golf had come a long way since the sticks and stones used in the 1400s. In 1618, a special golf ball was created, made of feathers instead of stone; it was called, understandably, the "Featherie." Featheries were so difficult to make that each one was often more expensive than a club! It was a relief to many golfers when less expensive balls were later mass-produced out of cheaper materials, like rubber.

By the 1700s, specially designed clubs and balls were being handcrafted by exclusive shops. The club handles were made mostly from special kinds of wood. Many early clubs also had heads made of wood, though some heads were made of blacksmith-forged iron. Today, most clubs are made entirely of lightweight, super-strong metal.

As the equipment improved, the game grew more and more popular. Larger tournaments became popular, and golf organizations opened around the world. In 1873, golf got a foothold in North America when golfers began a club in Canada. Fifteen years later, the United States caught golf fever and began a club in Yonkers, New York. This club started off very modest. In fact, its founders were called "The Apple Tree Gang" because their course, a small section of farmland, was filled with fruit trees. This didn't stop hundreds of eager golfers from flocking to the club, and then to the other clubs that started in the coming years.

In 1894, golf was a big deal in America. It was so big, in fact, that golfers formed the United States Golf Association, a group that created standardized rules for the game. The rules of American golf were unique to the country. However, they were based upon international guidelines, especially those of Scotland, the birthplace of the great game of golf.

 Questions

1 The author says people first created games using <u>makeshift equipment</u>. What does this mean?

    A   The equipment was durable.
    B   The equipment was special.
    C   The equipment was professional.
    D   The equipment was homemade.

 Tip

Remember that people first played golf with sticks and stones. What kind of equipment is this?

2 The author says that people spend so much time playing golf that they <u>shrugged off their obligation to train for the military</u>. What does this mean?

    A   They were not sure if they were supposed to train for the military.
    B   They did not bother to train for the military even though they were supposed to.
    C   They played games while they participated in the military.
    D   They were sent away to participate in the military.

 Tip

Go back and reread the paragraph. What were the people doing? What were they supposed to have been doing?

3 The passage says that the outlook for the new sport <u>brightened</u> again almost fifty years later, when King James IV discovered that the banned pastime was actually quite entertaining. What does <u>brightened</u> mean?

    A   Lit up
    B   Improved
    C   Opened
    D   Cheered up

Check your answers on the next page. Read the explanation after each answer choice.

Passage 4: "The Birth of Golf"

 Answers

1. D   The "equipment" was really sticks and stones that the people made into equipment. Therefore, the best answer choice is D.

2. B   The author means that people were so busy playing golf that they did not train for the military even though they were supposed to. Answer choice B is the best answer.

3. B   While all of the answer choices could be definitions of the word "brightened," in this passage, "brightened" means "improved."

Lesson 2: Summarizing

Standard 1C: Reading Comprehension

(1.8.15)   **Compare an original text to a summary to determine whether the summary accurately captures the key ideas.**

(1.8.16)   **Summarize a story of nonfiction passage or identify the best summary.**

(1.8.17)   **Identify the outcome or a conclusion of a story or nonfiction account, based on previous occurrences or events.**

(1.8.18)   **Identify the causes of events in a story of nonfiction account.**

How do you summarize?

When you summarize a piece of writing, you choose only the most important ideas. Summarization questions on ISAT may ask you to choose the best summary of a passage. To answer this type of question correctly, you need to select the answer choice that gives the main ideas of the passage, instead of just minor details.

You might also be asked to choose the best ending for a story or nonfiction passage based on what you have read. For this type of question, you will base your answers on the sequence of events in the story. For example, if you are reading a passage that tells how to plant sunflowers and the passage instructs you to plant the seeds in the ground, you can guess that the next step is probably to water the seeds.

Lastly, questions assessing this standard might also ask you to identify the causes of events in passages. In other words, these questions will ask you why something happened.

Activity

Read the following paragraph. Look for the main point as you read.

Ancient Egyptian physicians were very advanced for their time, but some of their "cures" for illnesses and diseases were way off base. While these physicians had some clinical knowledge, meaning they based some of their treatment on science, they were also very superstitious and offered their patients magical cures. If you lived in ancient Egypt and had a stomach ache, your doctor might tell you to crush a hog's tooth and put it inside of a sugar cake and eat it. To cure a headache, your doctor would advise you to fry a catfish skull in oil and rub this oil on your head. If you had trouble with your eyes, your physician would mix together special ingredients, including parts of a pig, put the mixture in your ear, and say, "I have brought this thing and put it in its place. The crocodile is weak and powerless."

Underline a sentence in this paragraph that summarizes its meaning. Then list two supporting details—details that should NOT be included in a summary—on the lines below.

1. _____

_____

2. _____

_____

Passages 1 and 2

Now read these passages and answer the questions that follow.

Passage 1

Wilson Bentley

Wilson Bentley once described a snowflake as a miracle of beauty and a masterpiece of design. Bentley was a farmer who lived in Jericho, Vermont. After many attempts at using a microscope and an early camera, he became the first person to photograph a snowflake. Bentley was a self-educated young man who accomplished this historic feat in 1885 when he was just twenty years old. He went on to capture images of more than five thousand individual snowflakes, not one of which was exactly alike.

During the long, cold winters in Vermont, Bentley braved the frigid temperatures in pursuit of the exquisite beauty of snow crystals. The task was daunting, considering that snowflakes are made of many individual snow crystals, which would melt in an instant and be lost forever. Bentley assembled his equipment outdoors in order to preserve the snow crystals and capture their images on glass plates. He did this hard work not for money, but for the sheer thrill of discovering yet another brilliant image.

Bentley submitted many of his photographs and a description of his work to the Smithsonian Institute in Washington, D.C. His manuscript was labeled as unscientific and was rejected. Hoping to share his findings with others, he sold individual glass plates to schools and colleges for five cents each. His work was later published by the U.S. Weather Bureau, *National Geographic*, and *Scientific American*.

Wilson Bentley's neighbors fondly referred to him as "Snowflake" Bentley. Understanding the fragile, fleeting life of a snowflake, Bentley once said that "when a snowflake melted, that design was forever lost. Just that much beauty was gone, without leaving any record behind." Thanks to the curiosity and ingenuity of Snowflake Bentley, there are records of thousands of snow crystals, each reflecting a beauty like no other.

Passage 2

The Art of a Snowflake

When the outside air temperature is below freezing, the landscape can be transformed by millions of snowflakes, which are actually made up of billions of snow crystals.

A snow crystal is a single crystal of frozen water, shaped in an elaborate lattice pattern. Each snow crystal is created with two molecules of hydrogen for each molecule of oxygen, which is indicated by the formula, H_2O. Snow crystals can be made up of only a few water molecules but are often made up of one thousand or more water molecules. Several snow crystals are usually stuck together to form what we commonly refer to as snowflakes.

Snow crystals are created when water molecules line up in tree-like branches called stellar dendrites, which are often arranged as a hexagon. Not all snow crystals are six-sided, however. If you looked under a microscope, you would sometimes see twelve-sided snow crystals or even crystals shaped like triangles. In frigid temperatures, like at the South Pole, a snow crystal resembles a solid beveled rectangle, just like a rectangular-shaped diamond cut for jewelry.

Whether a snow crystal is a hexagon, triangle, or rectangle, its shape is nearly always symmetrical, meaning each side is very much like the others. Snow crystals can grow along flat surfaces, referred to as faceting, or into more complex shapes, referred to as branching. The facets and branches of snow crystals are created at nearly the exact same time, under the exact same conditions, which is why each branch of a snow crystal is nearly symmetrical.

There is a difference between individual snow crystals and frozen rain. While still high in the atmosphere, snow crystals are formed into intricate patterns as water molecules condense on a microscopic piece of dust. Frozen rain, or sleet, consists of single drops of water that freeze while falling to the ground. A single frozen raindrop lacks the delicate shape of a snow crystal.

Freshly fallen snow appears white; yet frozen water is often transparent. If you look very closely at individual snow crystals, they, too, appear clear. However, when snowflakes fall to the ground, they are mixed with air, leaving spaces between the flakes. When light hits a multitude of snowflakes, it bounces around among the flakes, scattering individual colors, and gets reflected back as white light.

You've probably heard that no two snowflakes are alike. Scientists say, for the most part, that's true. Since each snowflake experiences changing weather conditions as it falls, each and every snow crystal grows differently depending on wind and temperature conditions at a given moment in time. Since snow crystals follow unique paths on the way to the ground, there really are no two snowflakes that are alike.

 Questions

1   Write a sentence summarizing "Wilson Bentley."

_____

_____

2   Write two sentences summarizing "The Art of a Snowflake."

_____

_____

3   In what way are the two passages alike?

_____

_____

Now check the sample answers on the next page.

Passages 1 and 2: "Wilson Bentley" and "The Art of a Snowflake"

 Answers

1. **Sample answer:** Wilson Bentley became the first person to photograph a snow flake, which wasn't easy since snowflakes melt very quickly.

2. **Sample answer:** Snowflakes are actually made of up snow crystals, which are often made up of thousands or more water molecules. Snow crystals grow and change depending on wind and temperature, so no two snowflakes are exactly alike.

3. **Sample answer:** The two passages are alike in that they discuss snowflakes and how they are beautiful but fleeting.

Passage 3

Read this passage and answer the questions that follow.

Excerpt from *The Canterville Ghost*
by Oscar Wilde

When Mr. Hiram B. Otis, the American Minister, bought Canterville Chase, everyone told him he was doing a very foolish thing, as there was no doubt at all that the place was haunted. Indeed, Lord Canterville himself, who was a man of the most punctilious honour, had felt it his duty to mention the fact to Mr. Otis when they came to discuss terms.

"We have not cared to live in the place ourselves," said Lord Canterville, "since my grandaunt, the Dowager Duchess of Bolton, was frightened into a fit, from which she never really recovered, by two skeleton hands being placed on her shoulders as she was dressing for dinner, and I feel bound to tell you, Mr. Otis, that the ghost has been seen by several living members of my family, as well as by the rector of the parish, the Rev. Augustus Dampier, who is a Fellow of King's College, Cambridge. After the unfortunate accident to the Duchess, none of our younger servants would stay with us, and Lady Canterville often got very little sleep at night, in consequence of the mysterious noises that came from the corridor and the library."

"My Lord," answered the Minister, "I will take the furniture and the ghost at a valuation. I have come from a modern country, where we have everything that money can buy; and with all our spry young fellows painting the Old World red, and carrying off your best actors and prima-donnas, I reckon that if there were such a thing as a ghost in Europe, we'd have it at home in a very short time in one of our public museums, or on the road as a show."

"I fear that the ghost exists," said Lord Canterville, smiling, "though it may have resisted the overtures of your enterprising impresarios. It has been well known for three centuries, since 1584 in fact, and always makes its appearance before the death of any member of our family."

"Well, so does the family doctor for that matter, Lord Canterville. But there is no such thing, sir, as a ghost, and I guess the laws of Nature are not going to be suspended for the British aristocracy."

"You are certainly very natural in America," answered Lord Canterville, who did not quite understand Mr. Otis's last observation, "and if you don't mind a ghost in the house, it is all right. Only you must remember I warned you."

Questions

1   Which is the best summary of this passage?

A   A British man proves to an American that there is no such thing as ghosts.
B   An American man buys a British mansion even though it's haunted.
C   Two men try to do business but are interrupted by nosy ghosts.
D   A skeleton puts its hands on the shoulder of an old woman.

 Tip

Choose the answer choice that includes the most important details. Eliminate answer choices that contain only details and not important information. Also eliminate answer choices that include only one important detail in the passage.

2   How does the Canterville family deal with the ghosts in their house?

A   By making friends with them
B   By ignoring them
C   By refusing to live there
D   By giving the house to Americans

 Tip

This question asks about a cause. What is the reason that Lord Canterville is selling the home? Reread the passage if you are unsure.

3   Which of the following should NOT be included in a summary of this passage?

A   Mr. Otis keeps reminding Lord Canterville that he's American.
B   Lord Canterville makes sure to explain that the house is haunted.
C   Lady Canterville often got very little sleep at night.
D   Mr. Otis insists that there is no such thing as ghosts.

Tip

This question is asking which answer choice should NOT be included. To answer this question correctly, choose the answer choice that is *least* important to the central idea of the passage.

Now check your answers on the next page.

Passage 3: "Excerpt from *The Canterville Ghost*"

 **Answers**

1. B   This passage focuses on an American man buying a mansion from a British man who insists that the property is haunted.

2. C   The Canterville family deals with the ghosts by refusing to live there. Lord Canterville explains this in the first line of the second paragraph.

3. C   All of the answer choices give important details about the story except answer choice C. The fact that Lady Canterville didn't sleep at night is just a small detail alluded to in the story. C is the best answer choice.

Passage 4

Read this passage and answer the questions that follow.

Mr. Salazar

Donning a new shirt and shorts and with his book bag on his back, Seth proceeded toward the bus stop. *The first day of school is always a blast*, Seth thought. He was eagerly anticipating seeing some of his friends that he wasn't able to touch base with over summer vacation while he worked with his grandfather on his farm.

Seth felt certain that eighth grade was going to be his best year ever. As one of the oldest students, he knew nearly everyone in the school. He was going to be on the varsity basketball team and might even be chosen as a starter. The best part, however, would be having Mr. Jordan as his homeroom teacher.

Mr. Jordan had been Seth's English teacher for several years and Seth really enjoyed his classes, mainly because Mr. Jordan had an incredible sense of humor and managed to make learning great fun. After the class had read a new short story or novel, he would match students to characters and have the students act out a chapter or two. While at first Seth thought this would be extremely corny and con-templated outright refusing to comply with it, he changed his mind when Mr. Jordan assigned him the role of an old woman in one of Flannery O'Connor's short stories. Seth tried in vain to raise his deep voice so it resembled an old woman's, but all he managed to do was squeak—and make his classmates crack up with riotous laughter. Then Mr. Jordan assigned Seth's friend Charlie the part of a desk, which required Charlie to be quiet, a seemingly impossible task. Once everyone had their parts, they managed to get through it without laughing too loudly. Mr. Jordan discussed character motivation by asking each student (except Charlie) what made their character do the things that he or she did. In Seth's perception, Mr. Jordan was in the running for one of the world's greatest teachers.

This is why Seth was completely distraught to discover another man standing in front of Mr. Jordan's desk. "Who's *that*?" he asked his friend Ashley. "And why is he in Mr. Jordan's classroom leaning on his desk?" Ashley shook her head and told Seth she had no clue. The man was much younger than Mr. Jordan and, even though he hunched his shoulders and leaned forward slightly, he was much taller—too tall, in Seth's opinion. The man slipped his hands into his pockets nervously and smiled an awkward, crooked smile. When Seth's eyes met his, he nodded, but Seth was too bewildered to respond.

When everyone entered the room, the man introduced himself as Mr. Salazar. "Are you a substi-tute?" called out someone from the back of class.

Mr. Salazar shook his head negatively. "Mr. Jordan and his wife relocated to Philadelphia about a month ago, and I have been bestowed the honor of being your teacher this year."

While some students clapped and welcomed Mr. Salazar, Seth was too stunned to respond. His whole mood was stifled by the thought: *No more Mr. Jordan?* That meant no more funny plays, no joking around in class—learning would no longer be enjoyable. This man did not resemble Mr. Jordan in the slightest. He looked serious, nervous, and much too young to be a teacher. "Is this the first class you've ever taught?" Seth inquired.

Mr. Salazar laughed. "Yes," he replied. "I graduated college last May, but I student-taught during my last year and learned a great deal. I'm going to teach you many new and interesting things and we're going to have lots of fun learning."

Yeah, right, Seth thought. *This is going to ruin everything.*

Seth and his friend Charlie made a beeline for the basketball court at recess. Seth was surprised to see Mr. Salazar on the court dribbling a basketball. His lanky frame moved surprisingly swiftly as he approached the hoop. He reached up and gently shot the ball—*swish*! Mr. Salazar stopped when he saw them. "Hey boys, would you like to play?" he inquired.

Seth and Charlie approached him as two more boys walked onto the court. "*You* play basketball?" Seth asked him, surprised that someone who seemed so awkward and gangly would be involved in athletics.

"You bet!" replied Mr. Salazar enthusiastically. "I played in both high school and college."

Seth caught the rebound and tried unsuccessfully to pass by Mr. Salazar. Seth chuckled. "For a too-tall dude, you can really move," he joked. Mr. Salazar knocked the ball away from Seth and sunk it into the hoop. A crowd of students gathered around the court to watch Mr. Salazar's incredible skills. Seth's classmates attempted to defeat him in a lopsided four-on-one match, but it was to no avail. Exhausted, Seth plopped down on the side of the court. "You're so tall, no one can beat you," Seth said.

"Nah," Mr. Salazar replied and sunk yet another basket without breaking a sweat. "Size doesn't have all that much to do with it. Some of the best players on my college team were only average height, if not smaller. It's how you maneuver that makes the difference."

"You are really awesome," Seth said. "You are *really* awesome. Could you teach us to move like that?"

"Sure!" said Mr. Salazar. "I'm going to teach you lots of things—and not just about basketball. We're going to start a new novel in English today called *Dogsong*. Have you ever heard of it?"

Dogsong was written by Gary Paulsen, Seth's favorite author. Seth told Mr. Salazar about the other books he had read by Paulsen. When the bell rang ending recess, Seth headed back to class excited for the first time since he'd arrived at school. Maybe his fears weren't warranted and things weren't so bad after all.

 Questions

1   Which is the best summary of this passage?

   A   A boy does not like his new teacher because he is too tall and has no teaching experience.

   B   A boy is upset to discover that his favorite teacher has moved to a different place and will no longer be teaching at the school.

   C   A boy is saddened to learn that his favorite teacher has moved, but then discovers that he likes his new teacher as well.

   D   A boy learns to like his new teacher, who likes to play basketball and read his favorite author.

 Tip

Choose the answer choice that tells what the *entire* passage is about.

2   Why did Seth like Mr. Jordan?

   A   He made learning fun.
   B   He knew how to play basketball.
   C   He liked to read Gary Paulsen.
   D   He had a great speaking voice.

 Tip

Reread the beginning of the passage if you don't remember the answer to this question.

3   Why was Seth surprised to learn that Mr. Salazar is good at basketball?

   A   Mr. Salazar does not seem the type to play.
   B   Mr. Salazar does not seem outgoing enough.
   C   Mr. Salazar seems to move awkwardly.
   D   Mr. Salazar seems too young to play well.

Tip

Think about Seth's first impression of Mr. Salazar. Then reread the end of the passage, where Seth watches Mr. Salazar play basketball.

Check your answers on the next page.

Passage 4: "Mr. Salazar"

 Answers

1. C This answer choice best summarizes what the entire passage is about. The beginning of the passage focuses on Mr. Jordan and the end tells why Seth likes Mr. Salazar. Both ideas are important to the central idea of the story.

2. A This question asks about a cause: why Seth liked Mr. Jordan. Seth liked Mr. Jordan because he has a good sense of humor and makes learning fun. Answer choice A is the best answer.

3. C At first Seth thinks that Mr. Salazar is too tall. Then he is surprised that someone so lanky can move so well. Answer choice C is the best answer.

Passage 5

Read the passage and answer the questions that follow.

The History of Drive-In Theaters
by Dale Stein

When people go to the movies they are often greeted by long lines at the ticket counter, expensive refreshments, and a sticky floor beneath their feet. One way to skip those aggravations and still enjoy the latest blockbuster hit is to go to a drive-in theater. Back in the late 1940s and 1950s, open-air cinemas, or "ozoners," peaked in popularity. Drive-in theaters were an inexpensive way for families to enjoy a movie in the comfort of their own vehicles. They could load the car with snacks, drinks, and blankets, and settle in a for a feature film on a warm summer night. They could talk, joke, and laugh in the privacy of their own car without the fear of being shushed by someone sitting a few rows back.

The First Drive-in Theater

The first drive-in theater was invented by Richard Hollingshead, a young sales manager from Camden, New Jersey, who wanted to create a way for people to enjoy movies from their cars. He experimented with this idea by mounting a movie projector on the hood of his car and aiming it at a white sheet attached to trees in his yard. Placing a radio behind the sheet for sound, he had the basic ideas for his open-air cinema in place, but Hollingshead strove to make it better. He worried that bad weather might affect the picture, so he used hoses and lawn sprinklers to simulate a rainstorm. The next problem he faced was parking. When one car parked right behind another, the view of the screen was partially blocked. By spacing the cars apart and parking the rear cars on blocks and ramps, Hollingshead discovered a way for all moviegoers to view the screen without a problem. With his idea perfected, Hollingshead obtained a patent for an open-air cinema on May 16, 1933, and less than one month later, he opened the first drive-in theater in Camden. Three large speakers broadcast sound while the screen displayed the picture. The cost for a drive-in movie was twenty-five cents for the car and twenty-five cents for each person.

An Uphill Climb for Drive-in Theaters

It didn't take long before other drive-in theaters were built. By 1942, there were about a hundred drive-in theaters across the United States, but World War II slowed this growth. Gasoline, rubber, and metal were all rationed for the war effort, and it wasn't until the war ended that the number of open-air cinemas increased. By 1948, the number of drive-in theaters had risen to 820.

A number of factors contributed to the rising popularity of drive-in theaters, one being the improved technology for sound. Gone were the days of bullhorn speakers mounted to the screen. Instead, drive-in theaters used in-car speakers that allowed moviegoers to adjust the volume to their liking. The baby boom also contributed to the popularity of open-air cinemas. In the years following World War II, mainly the 1940s and 1950s, there was a sharp increase in the number of babies born in the United States. As the number of families with children grew, outdoor cinemas became more family friendly. Theater owners built playgrounds where toddlers and young children could play before the movie started. Some cinemas became small amusement parks offering pony rides, train rides, miniature golf, talent shows, and of course, refreshments. By the end of the 1940s, open-air cinemas had surpassed indoor cinemas in popularity. They reached their peak in 1958 with more than four thousand outdoor screens showing movies across the country.

Cruising to the Concession Stand

Refreshment stands have long been a staple of the drive-in movie industry. Offering a variety of foods from hot dogs, hamburgers, and French fries, to assorted candy and beverages, refreshment stands were often responsible for a large amount of drive-in theaters' profits. In the early days, some outdoor cinemas had "carhops," waiters and waitresses who brought food right to your car window. Other cinemas went with a more traditional cafeteria-style refreshment stand, while some larger theaters offered restaurants with full meals. To increase refreshment sales even more, theaters began showing intermission trailers, or "clocks," between films. These trailers were short, ten- to twenty-minute, animated films featuring dancing snacks and drinks that enticed moviegoers to head to the concession stand. They often had a clock somewhere on the screen counting down the time to the start of the next film.

Drive-in Theaters Hit a Roadblock

Just as quickly as they rose to popularity, drive-in theaters began a downward slide. Through the 1960s their numbers remained fairly constant, but the audience changed. Fewer families attended drive-in movies, so cinemas began targeting a teen audience with movies unsuitable for young children. In the 1970s, property values began to increase and many theaters closed to make room for shopping centers. Large indoor theaters offered the newest movies on multiple screens, and outdoor cinemas suffered.

In addition, cable television and videocassette recorders (VCRs) were introduced. These inventions brought Hollywood movies into people's homes. They no longer had to drive to a theater, buy tickets and snacks, and find a place to park. They simply turned on the television or popped in a videotape. By 1983, there were less than three thousand drive-in theaters in the country.

Reversing the Trend

Throughout the 1990s, many open-air cinemas continued to close. Less than six hundred drive-in theaters and 815 screens remained in operation in the United States by 1997. Good news is on the horizon, however. In recent years, some drive-in theaters have reopened, new open-air cinemas have been built, and families are beginning to attend the outdoor pictures once again.

 Questions

1 Which is the best summary of the second paragraph of this passage?

A The first drive in was invented by Richard Hollingshead, who wanted to create a way for people to enjoy movies from their cars, but Hollingshead had to overcome many obstacles to perfect his idea.

B Richard Hollingshead obtained a patent for the first drive-in theater, an open-air cinema, on May 16, 1933, and opened the first theater only a month later.

C Richard Hollingshead invented the first drive-in theater by mounting a movie projector on the hood of his car and aimed it at a white sheet attached to trees in his year.

D The first drive-in theater had three large speakers that broadcast sound and a screen that displayed the picture.

 Tip

Choose the answer choice that summarizes the entire paragraph and not just part of the paragraph.

2 What happened in the 1960s that decreased the popularity of the drive-in theater?

A The audience changed.
B Cable television was introduced.
C Property values increased.
D VCRs were introduced.

 Tip

Reread the section "Drive-in Theaters Hit a Roadblock" to find the answer to this question.

3   Which is the best summary of this passage?

A   Inventing the drive-in theater was no easy task, but an inventor named Richard Hollingshead managed after much effort.

B   Once the first drive-in theater was built, many more drive-ins were built across the country.

C   Refreshment stands were an important part of the drive-in theater, as much of the theater's profits stemmed from refreshment sales.

D   While the drive-in theater has suffered many setbacks over the years, it might be making a comeback.

 Tip

Rereading the beginning and end of the passage may help you choose the best summary.

Now check your answers on the next page.

Passage 5: "The History of Drive-In Theaters"

 Answers

1. B   The second paragraph is mostly about Hollingshead inventing the drive-in theater. Answer choice B is the best answer.

2. A   In the 1960s, the audience changed. This hurt drive-in theaters. Popular movies for teens were not suitable for young children, which meant fewer families went to the drive-in.

3. D   Answer choice D best summarizes the central meaning of the entire passage.

Lesson 3: Comprehending Reading Strategies

Standard 1B: Reading Strategies

Standard 1C: Reading Comprehension

(1.8.06)   Make and verify predictions based on prior knowledge and understanding of genres.

(1.8.07)   Clarify an understanding of text by creating outlines, notes, or other visual representations.

(1.8.08)   Use information in charts, graphs, diagrams, maps, and tables to help understand a reading passage.

(1.8.09)   Compare the content and organization (e.g., themes, topics, text structure, story elements) of various selections.

(1.8.10)   Relate information in the passage to other readings.

(1.8.11)   Identify cause and effect organizational patterns in fiction and nonfiction.

(1.8.12)   Identify compare and contrast organizational patterns in fiction and nonfiction.

(1.8.13)   Identify proposition and support organizational patterns in fiction and nonfiction.

How Do You Comprehend Reading Strategies?

A piece of writing, whether it is a short sentence or a long book, may look simple. However, it may not be simple at all. A sentence can be much, much more than just a string of words. It may contain many important ideas and carry many special meanings. That's why it's important for readers to learn strategies for making the most of what they read. There are many kinds of reading strategies an effective reader should know.

Questions about reading strategies might ask you to use prior knowledge to help develop information in a passage. You might have to examine an author's use of comparison and contrast to learn more about a topic. You might have to explore cause-and-effect relationships to decide why certain events in a passage have occurred. You may also be asked to look at maps or charts, and understand the kinds of information they contain.

Activity 1

Determine which of the following is a cause and which is an effect. Write "cause" or "effect" in the right-hand column. Remember that a cause is something that happens. The effect is the result of the cause.

1.	A. It was icy outside.	
	B. I slipped and fell on the sidewalk.	
2.	A. The airplane landed.	
	B. The airplane reached its destination.	
3.	A. Many people use computers today.	
	B. Computers are useful for many tasks.	
4.	A. Millions of people think donuts are delicious.	
	B. Donuts are a popular snack.	

Activity 2

Pets Among Kelptown Students

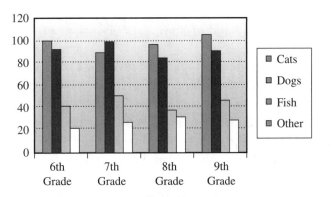

Look carefully at the chart above. It gives you many kinds of information. Make a list of all the types of information you can learn from this chart.

_____

_____

_____

_____

Passage 1

Now read this passage and answer the questions that follow.

Digging Up James Fort

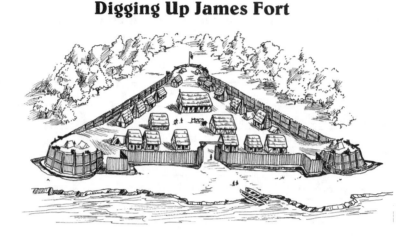

Archaeologist William Kelso had a shovel, a wheelbarrow, and a mission. He was determined to unearth the remains of James Fort, an early British settlement in America. Most archaeologists thought he would discover nothing but dirt. They believed that over the centuries the James River had washed away the land on which the fort had once stood. Kelso was in the minority who thought the fort, which he thought of as "an archaeological time capsule," could still be found.

Kelso received permission to begin an excavation on the 22-acre island in Virginia where the fort had been constructed in 1607. He commenced digging with his simple tools as local people gathered to observe him. Within hours, Kelso had found more evidence than he'd anticipated. He found metal buttons, armor and weapons, pieces of copper, animal bones, and fragments of dishes, pots, and pipes. Kelso had located a trash pit—an early kind of dump—of enormous proportions.

When he showed historians what he had found, they were astounded. A group of historians decided to give Kelso funding to continue his excavation. With that money, Kelso was able to hire a team of assistants and purchase better equipment. They found over four hundred thousand artifacts from the colonial years. One of their most important discoveries was not an artifact at all. In fact, to the untrained eye, this discovery looked just like black ink stains on the dirt. But Kelso knew that these stains represented the remains of the wooden walls of the fort. The team knew then that they hadn't just been digging in a nameless old dump. They had actually found the outline of two of James Fort's three walls, totaling two-hundred-and-fifty feet of logs. After uncovering the whole area between the walls, Kelso realized he had located the spot where the American government was first conceived, hundreds of years previously. He was soon to discover evidence, however, that that was not all that happened in James Fort.

The history of James Fort, and the whole area called Jamestown, is a terrible one. Only about one out of six people who moved there from England survived. The colony was characterized by power struggles, massacres, and starvation. Many historians believed that poor planning was the cause of these problems. When British leaders decided to colonize Jamestown, they did not carefully consider what type of citizens should immigrate there. Instead, they mostly sent aristocrats, servants, and craftspeople.

Few of these people knew how to grow their own food. The aristocrats were considered lazy and selfish and spent their time arguing over who should be in control of the colony. Furthermore, the British leaders who organized the colony were mostly concerned with finding gold. They encouraged the colonists to search for gold and barter with the Native Americans. "The colony's primary goal was to make a profit for the sponsors," Kelso wrote. This greedy goal left the colonists little time to improve their own community.

Kelso's discoveries contradicted some popular beliefs about what had happened in Jamestown. He discovered that the people of James Fort were not lazy. They had many tools that they used for their everyday tasks. Scattered around the fort and the trash pits were bullet molds, metal-working tools, glass-making tools, animal bones, weapons, fishhooks, and oyster shells. Researchers concluded that the colonists had hunted, fished, and made useful crafts.

Kelso's team also found lots of metal, especially copper, at the site. In the 1600s, the British had hoped that Native Americans would be impressed with metal tools and ornaments, since, most Native Americans relied on tools made of stone and wood. The Jamestown colonists expected to be able to trade copper to the natives for food and gold. However, some British sailors secretly sold copper directly to the Native Americans in the area. Because of this, the natives didn't need any more copper and didn't want to trade with the colonists. This was one of the primary factors in the downfall of James Fort.

The colonists continually struggled to find enough food. At first they relied on gifts of corn from nearby Native American villages. However, a severe drought caused most crops to die, and food became scarce all over Virginia; they called this "the starving time." The Native Americans could no longer afford to give food away. The Jamestown colonists were starving and desperate. They began attacking native villages in order to steal food. The natives in turn attacked the colonists, and surrounded James Fort. Trapped inside their fort, hundreds of colonists died of starvation and disease. Kelso's team found a hastily made cemetery full of Jamestown's most unfortunate residents.

The early years of Jamestown were a tragic failure, but they gave many people hopes for new opportunities in America. Jamestown went on to become the first capitol of Virginia. Soldiers camped there in the Revolutionary and Civil Wars. Thousands of new colonists immigrated to the area to begin new lives, having learned valuable lessons from the hardships that had taken place in James Fort.

 Questions

1   Complete the chart below by writing three events from the passage that occurred between the two that are shown.

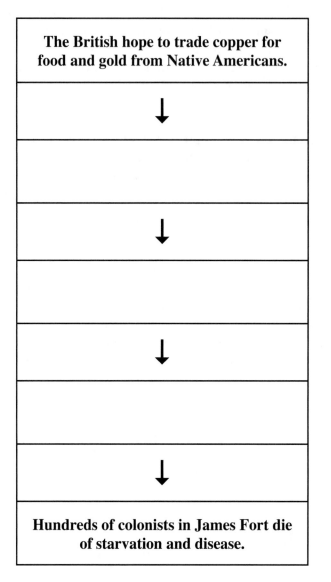

The British hope to trade copper for food and gold from Native Americans.
↓
↓
↓
↓
Hundreds of colonists in James Fort die of starvation and disease.

2   Why did archaeologists think Kelso wouldn't find anything during his excavation?

_____

_____

_____

_____

3   Which sentence from the passage supports the idea that Kelso's discoveries differed from some popular beliefs about what had happened in Jamestown?

_____

_____

_____

_____

4   How were later colonists in Jamestown different from the original settlers at James Fort?

_____

_____

_____

_____

Now check the sample answers on the next page.

Passage 1: "Digging Up James Fort"

 Answers

1. **Sample answer:** British sailors secretly sell copper to the Native Americans. Colonists rely on nearby Native American villages for food. A drought causes many crops to die and Native Americans will no longer trade food. Starving colonists attack Native American villages for food. Natives then attacked James Fort.

2. **Sample answer:** Most archaeologists believed that the James River had washed away any remnants of James Fort that may have existed.

3. **Sample answer:** "He found out that the people of James Fort were not lazy."

4. **Sample answer:** Later settlers had learned valuable lessons from the first settlers. They knew they would face hardships in Jamestown. They knew that they would have to concentrate on farming and improving their community if they wanted to survive.

Passage 2

Now read this passage and answer the questions that follow.

Going for Water
by Robert Frost

THE well was dry beside the door,
And so we went with pail and can
Across the fields behind the house
To seek the brook if still it ran;
Not loth to have excuse to go,
Because the autumn eve was fair
(Though chill), because the fields were ours,
And by the brook our woods were there.
We ran as if to meet the moon
That slowly dawned behind the trees,
The barren boughs without the leaves,
Without the birds, without the breeze.
But once within the wood, we paused
Like gnomes that hid us from the moon,
Ready to run to hiding new
With laughter when she found us soon.
Each laid on other a staying hand
To listen ere we dared to look,
And in the hush we joined to make
We heard, we knew we heard the brook.
A note as from a single place,
A slender tinkling fall that made
Now drops that floated on the pool
Like pearls, and now a silver blade.

 Questions

1   Why did the people in the poem go in search of the brook?

    A   They needed to follow it to find their way home.
    B   They wanted to take a quick swim to cool off.
    C   They needed water and the well near the house was dry.
    D   They wanted to gaze at the brook in the moonlight.

 Tip

Read the poem carefully before you make your choice. What did the people in the poem take with them when they went in search of the brook?

2   What do the drops in the pool of water look like?

    A   A silver blade
    B   Pearls
    C   Diamonds
    D   Moonlit leaves

 Tip

If you're not sure of the correct answer, read the poem again.

3   What will the people in the poem probably do next?

    A   Splash each other with cold water from the brook
    B   Lie next to the brook and gaze at the moon
    C   Get water from the brook and head for home
    D   Drink from the brook and continue on their journey

 Tip

Think carefully about the information given in the poem. Why did the people in the poem go in search of the brook in the first place?

4   How does this poem compare to other poems you have read? Use information from the poem and your own experience to support your answer.

_____

_____

_____

_____

 # Tip

Before you answer, try to recall some other poems you have read. How is this poem like other poems you have read?

Now check your answers on the next page.

Passage 2: "Going for Water"

 Answers

1. C   The first few lines of the poem indicate that the well beside the door was dry and that they set out through the field with a pail and a can to see if they could find the brook.

2. B   According to the last few lines of the poem, the drops in the pool look like pearls. Answer choice B is correct.

3. C   The people in the poem will probably fill their pails with water from the brook and then return to their house. According to the poem, the reason they went in search of the brook in the first place was because the well near the house was dry.

4.   **Sample answer:** This poem is similar to other poems I have read in many ways. First, many of the lines in this poem rhyme, and the poem itself has a rhythm. Like other poems, this poem includes a lot of imagery, as if the poet is painting a picture in your mind. It uses literary devices, such as similes and personification, to make the poem come alive. In addition, poets often express their feelings about a subject in their poetry. This poem expresses the poet's feelings about the brook and going to fetch the water.

Passage 3

Now read this passage and answer the questions that follow.

A Real Job

Damen Munez carefully explained his current predicament to his mother: he was in the midst of a financial crisis—in other words, he had no money. He was off school for nearly two weeks for spring break and desperately wanted a temporary job to earn some money to put toward a new bike he had seen in a store window. "Even though I'm extremely responsible and bright," Damen explained and held his hands in front of him dramatically, "I'm only thirteen and no one on Earth will give me a chance."

Gabriella Munez raised her eyebrows at her son and smiled. "What about me?" she asked. "You can work at the office this coming week. We have a huge deadline around the corner and could really use some extra help."

Damen could barely contain his excitement upon hearing his mother's words. "You want me . . . to work for you . . . at the office? I would ab-so-lute-ly love that—and you won't be sorry. I will work incredibly hard, I promise, and I will make you proud of me," Damen said.

His mother kissed him on the forehead. "I am already proud of you," she said, "but I think a real job would be a great experience. You can start on Monday."

Damen's mother was a book producer. She ran a small company that wrote and edited textbooks for publishers. Ever since they were little, Damen and his sister, Maria, had spent several hours each day at their mother's office, which had a kitchen in the back with a table where they completed their homework while enjoying a snack. Damen and Maria were fascinated with the many simultaneous projects their mother and her staff worked on and they loved being around creative individuals, hundreds of books, and modern computers and software. Damen had always wanted to work at his mother's company, but he never dreamed it would happen so soon. His mother had just given him a precious gift: a chance to use his outstanding writing skills to earn a paycheck. Damen contemplated his first assignment—he was a math whiz, so he figured he would probably be assigned to write a math textbook. He also loved to write science-fiction stories. Perhaps he would be writing a few of these, too.

When Damen and his mother arrived at the office Monday morning, the staff welcomed him aboard as their new "editorial assistant" and he felt truly honored. He had known most of the editors for many years, but he had never been allowed to work with them before.

Damen's mother explained that Matthew, an editor, needed some help fact-checking a social studies textbook. "I will check in with you before 1:00," she said, "when Grandma will pick you up."

"What?!" Damen scoffed. "Why can't I work the whole day, like you and the other editors?"

Gabriella chuckled. "You will be tired by 1:00, señor, just you wait and see," she said.

Matthew politely guided Damen to a table in his office and spread out the materials he would need for his first assignment: a printout of the textbook from the designer, a pen, and a computer with a CD in it. Matthew explained that Damen was to verify each highlighted fact in the textbook on the CD and if it wasn't available on the CD, Damen was to check it online. *This is a piece of cake*, Damen thought—until he saw the number of highlighted facts on each page. "I'm supposed to check every one of these?" he asked Matthew, who just smiled and nodded.

Damen quickly realized that verifying each fact was no easy task. He could verify some information easily on the CD, but other facts, like the dates for major events in Mesopotamia, had to be verified online using only credible university Web sites, which made his task even more daunting.

After about an hour, Damen asked Matthew if he could take a break and stretch and Matthew agreed that this was a good idea. Damen headed downstairs to the kitchen, where his mother was stirring milk in her coffee. Damen told his mother about his work and asked if there was any way possible he could switch to an assignment requiring writing, but she just grinned. "You have to learn to walk before you can run, Damen," she explained, "and besides, work is just that—work—and you have to learn to do what needs to be done without complaint."

Damen reluctantly returned to his workstation and continued his task. Every so often he would look and up and see the other editors typing quickly, answering phone calls, and walking from office to office with folders and books. He wondered how they managed to complete tedious tasks, like the one he was doing, while still managing to be creative when necessary. He also wondered how they could keep track of so many things at once without losing their sanity. They made their jobs look easy, but Damen was realizing that being an editor was actually very difficult.

When the clock struck one, Damen had a headache, his eyes were blurry, his back ached, he had ink all over his hands, and his stomach was growling. Frustrated, he told Matthew that he had only managed to verify the facts in the first few chapters of the book. "That's good!" exclaimed Matthew. "You're a great help. You can pick up where you left off tomorrow."

When Damen descended the stairs, his mother was waiting for him. "Mom," he said, "I don't think I did so well. I had to fact-check a social studies book and I don't think I got as much done as I should have."

"Did you do a good job?" asked his mother.

Damen explained that he knew the facts he had checked were correct, but that it was very tedious and difficult work.

Mrs. Munez raised her eyebrows. "Ah," she said. "You're not quitting, are you?"

"No!" Damen replied. "I'm just trying to figure out how I can do a better job tomorrow."

Mrs. Munez smiled and told Damen that she was very proud of him. "If I didn't know you and you were hired as an editorial assistant here and had such a positive attitude, I'd be thrilled," she said.

 Questions

1   What causes Damen to think he did a bad job?

   A   He had to verify many facts online.
   B   His mother will not give him a chance to write.
   C   His mother tells him he is leaving at 1:00.
   D   He has taken a long time to do his work.

 Tip

   In the passage, something causes Damen to feel that he hasn't done well. If you don't remember why he feels that way, look back to the passage.

2   How does Damen's first day on the job differ from what he expected?

   A   He was asked to write a science fiction story.
   B   He was not as tired as he thought he'd be.
   C   He was allowed to stay for the full day.
   D   He was not assigned to write a math textbook.

 Tip

   Think about Damen's expectations about his new job. Then, think about what he actually experienced. How did his experiences differ from his expectations?

3   How do you feel about having, or getting, your first job? How do you think your ideas about jobs might differ from reality? Use information from the passage to explain your answer.

_____

_____

_____

_____

Now check your answers on the next page.

Passage 3: "A Real Job"

 Answers

1. B   At the end of the story, Damen is ashamed because he feels that he didn't accomplish much during his shift. He only fact-checked a few chapters of the book.

2. D   Damen expected that, because he is good at math, he'd be assigned the task of writing a math textbook on his first day. This idea proved to be unrealistic.

3.   **Sample answer:** I don't have a job now, but I'd be excited to get one. Like Damen, I could use some spending money. He wants a new bike, but I'd like money for other things, like movie tickets and snacks. I would like to get a job which would let me do outdoor activities, even if it's just mowing lawns. Right now I think it sounds like fun to work outside and get paid for it. However, when I'm actually out there mowing people's grass, I may realize that the work is difficult and the summer sun is very warm. It would be like Damen realizing that editors' work is hard and tiring.

Passage 4

Now read this passage and answer the questions that follow.

The Emerald Isle

Known for its rolling green landscape, rainy climate, and rich history, there is an island about the size of West Virginia that sits in the Atlantic Ocean and is often referred to as the "Emerald Isle." Its borders also touch the Celtic Sea and the Irish Sea, and its capital is Dublin. This island is the country called Ireland.

The island of Ireland is separated into two parts. The southern part of the country is called the Republic of Ireland, and the northern part is suitably referred to as Northern Ireland. Northern Ireland is part of the United Kingdom, a group of countries on another nearby island, including England, Scotland, and Wales, as well as a few smaller islands. While Northern Ireland is governed under British laws, the Republic of Ireland, the southern part of the island, is independent.

Much of Ireland's coast is lined with low mountains, while the middle of the island is a combination of flat plains and rolling wetlands. Ireland's landscapes have been the focus of many paintings and poems. Because water-laden coastal winds cause the weather to be very rainy all year, the country is famous for its wetlands, called bogs, where many different plants grow in rich shades of green, including many different types of clovers. According to ancient Irish history, finding a four-leaf clover hidden among the regular three-leafed variety is said to be lucky. The Irish countryside, which includes farmlands as well as bogs, is often enclosed in a dense white fog.

The earliest Irish were primarily farmers, who struggled to produce enough food to feed their families and pay farmland rent to their British landlords. Around the year 1600, the potato crop was introduced to Irish farmers, who instantly loved the potato because

it thrived in many different conditions and could feed many, many people. The potato became the most widespread food in Ireland, and its abundance enabled the population to grow. Then, in 1845, a deadly fungus spread through most of Ireland's potato crops, causing them to rot and turn black. The Irish people lost their main source of food, and the famine continued for years, causing many people to die of starvation. Some tried to eat different types of plants and grasses, while others left the country and made new lives in Canada and America, causing Ireland's population to drop drastically.

Today, Ireland has developed a healthy population of around four million. The Irish diet now includes more than just the potato, though spuds are still a popular part of many meals. Ireland is known for its stews and other dishes made from beef, lamb, and pork, often accompanied by cabbage, onions, carrots, and thick breads. Most Irish foods are warm, comforting, and perfect to eat on wet and chilly days. The Irish also pass time on rainy days with music, often played on the traditional harp, fiddle, and bagpipes, as well as dances, including the Irish jig, which has an interesting history. When Ireland fell under British rule, the British outlawed everything traditionally Irish and imposed British customs—including music and dance—on the Irish people. This meant that performing dances to Irish music was illegal. Some bagpipers were even arrested! The Irish cherished their own music and dances, and so they began to perform them in secret. Irish dance masters traveled around the countryside, residing with different families and teaching their dances to many Irish citizens so that the dances would not be forgotten. They danced the jig in farm fields, on roads, at secret schools, and even in kitchens on tabletops. They invented new dance steps and sometimes participated in secret dance competitions, where the dance master who knew the most steps would win. Sometimes a dancer's skill was tested when he was asked to perform on top of a wobbly barrel. Now the jig is performed in many different public places, and anyone can learn the steps to this famous dance.

Ireland is also known for its castles, many of which can be found in Dublin, the country's capital city. Ireland's castles are impressively large and have existed for hundreds of years. Citizens and tourists can walk through their magnificent gardens and explore the majestic castles, many of which still have furniture and other antique items belonging to their former residents. The Dublin Castle was built in the early 1200s and was home to many British leaders until as recently as 1922. The Malahide Castle, located on the seaside, is even older than the Dublin Castle and was home to members of the same family for almost 800 years. Other historic buildings in the capital city include large government buildings, an ancient prison that is no longer used, churches (called abbeys), and former homes of famous Irish writers and other artists.

Another immediate association with Ireland is the country's national holiday, Saint Patrick's Day. Saint Patrick was born around the year 385 CE, and at this time, the Irish were a pagan people, meaning that they didn't belong to an established religion such as Christianity, Judaism, or Islam. Saint Patrick was a pagan until he reached the age of sixteen when he decided to become a Christian. He then became a bishop and set out to spread Christianity throughout Ireland, building churches and schools where the religion could be taught. He spread Christianity for thirty years before

his death, and two hundred years after he started, most of Ireland was Christian. A famous story of Irish folklore tells how Saint Patrick gave a sermon from a hillside and drove all the snakes from Ireland, which is intended to explain why no snakes exist in Ireland today. While snakes probably never lived in Ireland, the story represents the banishment of paganism from the country.

Saint Patrick's Day is celebrated on March 17th because it is said that this was the date of Saint Patrick's death. While it is Ireland's national holiday, Saint Patrick's Day is also celebrated in America, Canada, Australia, Russia, Japan, and other places around the world. The Irish holiday was once solely one of religious worship, but has expanded to include festivities such as parades, fireworks, concerts, and much more. Interestingly enough, it is said that the first Saint Patrick's Day parade took place in 1700s America, when Irish soldiers marched through New York City in celebration of the patron saint of Ireland. Today, the holiday is very popular in America as well as Ireland.

Questions

1   According to the map and the passage, where is the city of Castlebar located?

    A   The United Kingdom
    B   Northern Ireland
    C   Southern Ireland
    D   The Republic of Ireland

Tip

To answer this question correctly, you need to look at the map and skim over the article. Where is Castlebar?

2   What caused the Irish famine?

    A   A lack of work
    B   A drought
    C   A deadly fungus
    D   A change in rulers

Tip

Reread the section of the passage that discusses the Irish famine. What was its main cause?

3   What is one difference between the Dublin Castle and the Malahide Castle?

    A   The Dublin Castle is larger.

    B   The Malahide Castle is older.

    C   The Malahide Castle is unoccupied.

    D   The Dublin Castle is located in Britain.

 Tip

    If you're not sure of the answer, look back to the passage where these two castles are discussed.

4   The author of the article informs readers about many different aspects of Ireland.

    • If you were to travel to Ireland, what do you think you would like most?

    • What part of Irish culture would you like to learn more about?

Use details and information from the story in your answer.

_____

_____

_____

_____

 Tip

    Use what you've just read, along with what you already knew, to answer this question.

Now check your answers on the next page.

Passage 4: "The Emerald Isle"

 Answers

1. D   If you look at the map, the city of Castlebar is to the north, but not located in Northern Island, which the passage says is part of the United Kingdom and under British rule. Answer choice B says Southern Ireland. While this is true, this part of Ireland is not called Southern Ireland. It is called the Republic of Ireland, so answer choice D is the best answer.

2. C   A deadly fungus that killed off the potato crops in Ireland caused the famine. Answer choice C is the correct answer.

3. B   According to the passage, the Malahide Castle is older than the Dublin Castle.

4.   **Sample answer:** If I were to travel to Ireland I think I would appreciate the scenery the most. The article says that it rains often in Ireland and the landscape is a lush green. I think this would be beautiful. I would like to learn more about the castles in Ireland. They sound as if they're very beautiful and an important part of Ireland's history.

Lesson 4: Interpreting Instructions

Standard 1C: Reading Comprehension

(1.8.23)   **Determine whether a set of technical, multiple-step instructions or procedures are clear (e.g., if not clear, edit to clarify).**

Instructional Reading

Stories, poems, and books aren't the only reading materials we read on a regular basis. Most people also read instructions. These instructions might be about building a bookshelf, learning to ski, or using a new computer. Regardless of what the instructions are about, it's important to read and interpret them effectively.

On the ISAT, these types of questions might ask you to judge whether a set of instructions is complete and clear or not. If the instructions could be improved upon, you may be asked to decide what improvements should be made. Other questions may ask you about the structure and details of the instructions, or why the author wrote them.

Activity

The following is a sample set of instructions on how to make a building material called papier-mâché. Read the instructions and then answer the questions that follow.

How to Make Papier-mâché

1. Rip newspapers into tiny shreds.

2. Mix one part flour and one part water to form glue.

3. Soak the newspaper shreds in the glue.

4. Spread the newspaper shreds over the wire framework.

5. Let the glue dry along the framework.

6. Sandpaper the papier-mâché sculpture until it is smooth.

7. Paint as desired.

What materials are needed to make papier-mâché? Write them on the chart below.

_____

_____

_____

_____

_____

_____

What helpful information can be added to these instructions?

Passage 1

Now read this passage and answer the questions that follow.

How to Inflate the Water Wizard R-3 Raft

Boating is one of America's most beloved outdoor sports, but not everyone is able to store and transport a wooden or metal boat. If you want to ride this nation's beautiful waterways without lugging around a heavy, expensive boat, a Water Wizard raft may be just right for you! Rafts are inflatable boats; when properly filled with air, rafts are just as strong and durable as wooden or metal boats. When the air is removed, the deflated rafts are small enough to be easily stored in closets or cabinets.

Rafting is a great activity for people of all ages, if proper safety procedures are followed. Children should not raft without adult supervision, and it's important to follow these guidelines in order to make your Water Wizard raft safe for a long, enjoyable trip in your local lake or river.

Equipment:

- Water Wizard R-3 Raft
- An air pump (manual or electric)
- Patch kit (included with raft)
- Paddles (sold separately)
- Life vests and safety equipment

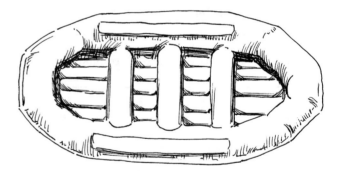

NOTE: Be sure to check all local laws to make sure you can operate a raft legally in your area. In some places, rafts need to be registered with local authorities before they can be used.

Once you've gathered the necessary items, take them to the site where you plan to launch the raft. Find a flat area, preferably dry and grassy, and unroll the deflated raft. Be sure to carefully flatten out any wrinkles to allow air to flow into the raft. At this point, the raft should look like a long, flat pancake—but not for long.

Note that the Water Wizard R-3 is made of two separate airbags. The raft is designed this way for greater safety. In case one airbag is damaged, the other will keep the raft afloat. The first airbag covers the "floor" of the raft. The second airbag is the "wall" of the raft. Each of these airbags needs to be pumped full of air.

Now that the raft is flattened out, find the intake valve for Airbag 1. The intake valve is a small rubber nozzle with a seal on it. After you find the intake valve, pull the seal out. Next, insert the hose from the air pump snugly into the open valve. Make sure no air escapes while you begin pumping. Within a few pumps, you should see the "floor" of the raft begin to fill with air. Continue pumping until Airbag 1 is solid. Then, quickly remove the air pump hose and re-seal the intake valve.

Locate the intake valve for Airbag 2. Repeat the actions taken to inflate Airbag 1.

Now that both airbags are pumped full of air, carefully feel the floor and walls of the raft to make sure they are solid to the touch. If the raft is soft, that means there is not enough air inside and you should use the pump to add more. Also, pause and listen for sounds. A hissing sound may indicate that air is escaping through a small hole in the raft. If any holes in the raft are detected, use the patch kit included with the Water Wizard R-3 to repair them. (Follow the directions included in the patch kit.)

Now, your raft is ready for launching! Carry the raft to the bank of the lake or river, being careful not to drag it across any rocks or tree branches that might cause damage. Then, insert the paddles into the oarlocks in the sides of the raft.

Enjoy your day on the water!

Questions

1   Why do you think the author included the "Note" in this passage?

_____

_____

_____

_____

2   Why did the author probably choose not to explain how to repair a hole in the raft?

_____

_____

_____

_____

3   According to the passage, why should you flatten out wrinkles in the raft before inflating it?

_____

_____

_____

_____

4   What other information could the author provide about how to safely operate the raft?

_____

_____

_____

_____

Now check the sample answers on the next page.

Passage 1: "How to Inflate the Water Wizard R-3 Raft"

 Answers

1. **Sample answer:** The author added a "Note" to this passage to show information that is important to rafters. This information is kept separate from the rest of the passage because it's not related to inflating the raft.

2. **Sample answer:** The author tells how to find holes in the raft and says, to fix holes, you should follow the directions included in the patch kit. Since rafters probably won't have to fix holes each time they inflate their raft, detailed instructions on fixing holes probably belong in a separate passage.

3. **Sample answer:** The author says that, after unrolling the raft on the ground, you should flatten out wrinkles in the raft. This allows air that is pumped into the raft to move freely through the raft.

4. **Sample answer:** Some other useful information that the author could have provided would be how many people could safely fit into the raft at the same time.

Passage 2

Now read this passage and answer the questions that follow.

Testing the Temperatures

Temperature means more to our world than whether we feel hot in the summer or cold in the winter. In fact, heat and cold are forces that help shape the planet. They provide energy that is constantly affecting our lives and our surroundings. Temperature works in ways that sometimes seem strange to us. You can demonstrate some of the interesting concepts of temperature easily, using just a few ordinary household items.

Demonstration 1: Heat Moves

An adult may have scolded you to close the door in the winter to keep the heat inside the house. This is because heat is constantly in motion. But it doesn't just flow in and out of houses. Heat also enters and leaves your body. You can demonstrate this idea with a very simple experiment.

What You Need:
3 Large Bowls
Water

Place the bowls in front of you on a table. Then, fill one bowl with very cold water. Fill the middle bowl with lukewarm water, which should be about room temperature. Fill the last bowl with water that's hot, but not hot enough to burn you.

Now, dunk your right hand into the cold water and your left hand into the hot water. Hold your hands like that for two minutes or so, until your hand feels accustomed to the temperature of the water. Then, quickly, remove your hands from the bowls and dunk them both into the center, lukewarm bowl.

What your hands feel in there may surprise you. You won't feel lukewarm water; instead, your right hand will feel hot and your left hand will feel cold. That's just the opposite of the temperatures they were just exposed to.

This strange reaction occurs because, in the lukewarm water, heat moves from your left to your right hand. The heat leaves your left hand to warm up the water, which makes your hand feel cold. Your cold right hand gathers up the heat quickly, and feels hot.

Demonstration 2: Heat Causes Movement

We know that heat is used to move things, from steam engines to hot-air balloons. However, heat moves a lot more than that. When heat comes in contact with the tiny molecules that make up all things, the heat makes the molecules begin to spin around quickly. This is what causes melting, for instance. You can demonstrate this with one of the easiest experiments you may ever do.

What You Need:
Ice cubes
A candle

Light the candle and place it near the ice cubes. The heat of the fire will transfer into the ice cubes and cause the molecules within to begin moving around. When these molecules begin spinning quickly, the ice cube will suddenly not be big enough to hold all the motion. It will expand—but it will still need more space. The molecules will begin to spin so quickly that they can't even maintain the shape of the ice cube anymore. The shape begins to break down, giving the molecules more space to move. This is why some things melt.

Before ending the demonstration, look at the candle. Wax will probably have melted from the candle. This is a double demonstration. When the molecules of the solid candle were heated by the fire, they spun so fast that the candle began breaking down, forming liquid wax. This wax will harden again when the heat, and the spinning, is reduced.

Demonstration 3: Hot and Cold Compete

Sometimes heat and cold are hard at work in the same place at the same time. They don't always mix, and this can lead to some unusual situations. To show one of these odd instances, you can try this fun little experiment.

What You Need:
An ice cube
A thin wire
Two small weights (such as rocks)

Attach the two small weights to the ends of the wire. Then, place the wire along the top of the ice cube. Before you know it, the wire will begin to cut through the ice, which is unusual enough—but the ice will reform around it! The ice will literally repair itself as it is cut.

The reason this happens is that the weights pull down on the wire. When the wire is placed over the ice cube, the pull causes pressure. Pressure leads to heat, which melts the ice. However, the heat is slight, and most of the ice is still very cold. So, just after any of the ice melts, the coldness of the rest of it causes it to freeze again.

 Questions

1   Why does the author list instructions for three demonstrations?

    A   The demonstrations should be done at the same time.
    B   The demonstrations each show important concepts of temperature.
    C   The demonstrations all use the same materials.
    D   The demonstrations must be done in this particular order.

 Tip

Think about the information you've just read. What makes these three sets of instructions fit well together?

2   What does the author emphasize about each of these demonstrations?

    A   They require many tools.
    B   They can be expensive.
    C   They are easy to do.
    D   They are difficult to accomplish.

 Tip

What do the three demonstrations have in common? If you need a hint, look back to the passage.

3   If an illustration were to be added to Demonstration 2, what would it most likely show?

    A   How an ice cube expands and melts
    B   How people operate hot-air balloons
    C   How to light a candle
    D   How steam engines work

 Tip

Skim over the information about the second demonstration in this passage. What is it mostly about?

4   What extra information would be most helpful in the instructions for Demonstration 3?

    A   The weight of the rocks

    B   The strength of the wire

    C   The amount of pressure

    D   The temperature of the ice

Tip

Look back to Demonstration 3. What added information would you want to have before starting this demonstration?

Now check your answers on the next page.

Passage 2: "Testing the Temperatures"

 Answers

1. B   These demonstrations are grouped together because they share a theme. They each show an important concept of temperature.

2. C   The author states several times that these demonstrations are special because of their simplicity. They are very easy to do. Answer choice C is the best answer.

3. A   Demonstration 2 is mostly about melting. An illustration of how an ice cube expands and then melts would be most helpful.

4. A   The weight of the rocks would be the most helpful information. The author says to use "small weights" such as rocks. However, people may have differing ideas of what is or isn't small.

Passage 3

Now read this passage and answer the questions that follow.

Beating Writer's Block

Imagine a boy sitting at his classroom desk, switching on an electronic word processor, or placing an empty pad of paper in front of him. He has at his disposal the instruments for writing—a pencil, pen, or a computer keyboard—and he is motivated to write, and yet he doesn't . . . or just can't.

The minutes tick by, and the boy stares at the empty paper or screen. He feels puzzled by his inability to organize his words and ideas, and then he becomes frustrated, which makes it even harder to think clearly. He jots down a few words and then, grumbling, erases them. Hours pass and he still hasn't accomplished anything.

Are you familiar with this sort of scenario? If you are, then you've experienced writer's block. This is a frustrating phenomenon that affects many potential writers. It restrains their creativity, keeps their productivity low, and generally makes writing a miserable chore. However, examining this confounding problem and some ways to reduce its effect on you can make writing enjoyable again.

Writer's block may have many easily understood causes, including tiredness or lack of fresh ideas. It may also have more underlying causes, like ugly emotions such as self-doubt. You may feel like you are incapable of writing anything valuable or that you could stare at the paper or screen for months without producing anything worthwhile. You may start to feel that writing is just not worth all the hassle.

Regardless of the cause, writer's block typically carries along feelings of panic, dissatisfaction, frustration, and additional self-doubt. Maybe the scariest thing about writer's block is that it seems to regenerate itself. The more blocked up your words are, the worse you feel about it—the worse you feel about it, the more your words block up!

So, your objective is to discover a method of breaking that gloomy cycle. Initially, you should think about other factors in your life that might be bothering you. These factors may be completely unrelated to writing (like failing a math test or arguing with a friend) that are clouding your thoughts. Working on a remedy to that concern may reduce your writer's block, as well as improve the rest of your daily life.

If the roots of your writer's block are simpler, then the solutions will likely also be simpler. There are dozens of fun, easy ways to kick writer's block out of your schedule!

Here's a scenario you may recognize: you have a writing assignment due early the next morning, but you haven't been able to get a grip on it yet. You're becoming frustrated and anxious as the hours pass but the paper remains empty. The first thing to do is remind yourself that negative feelings like frustration and anxiety are only going to add to your burden. When your brain is relaxed, you can then focus on getting your writing done right.

You've probably heard of "brainstorming," one useful tactic for dealing with writer's block. To brainstorm, just use a separate paper and scribble down whatever ideas come to mind. It may help to start by writing down your topic, and then making a simple diagram to show ideas related to that topic. If your topic was anacondas, you might write "anacondas" and then draw lines that connect concepts like "What they look like," "What they eat," "Where they live," and so on.

If you're capable of choosing or modifying your topic, be sure it's something you're interested in. You probably wouldn't be too enthusiastic about writing an essay on the history of socks! Choose something that excites your mind, because if you're excited about writing, the reader will likely be more excited to read.

You may face a situation in which you need to choose your own topic, but you just can't think of anything. That can even be worse than having an assigned topic that you dislike. There are ways of resolving this problem, though. Let's say you are assigned to write a short story about a topic of your choice. You can't quite think of anything you want to write about. It seems like all the good topics have already been used up. When you start to feel like this, it's time to take action.

One great step you can take would be to use writing exercises. Just as you might jog, swim, or do push-ups to exercise your muscles, you can also give your writing ability a work-out. There are many ways you can do this, and most of them are easy and fun.

For instance, you might find your topic for the short story by looking at pictures. Find a book with illustrations, a photo album, or even a painting hanging on a wall. Then, just think about it! Ask questions about what's taking place in the picture. Who or what is in the picture? Why was the picture taken? What do the colors (or lack of colors) mean? How did the creator get the idea for this picture? Each of these questions will give you some ideas. It's amazing how much you can learn visually that can help you work verbally.

Here's another, similar idea: Gather up some old magazines and newspapers. Read through them and cut out any item you find interesting. Cut out pictures, names, and headlines, and then gather them into piles. Without looking, pick out a picture, a name, and a headline, and then try to make a story that connects all three. This can be a fun exercise, and the results may be surprising.

Sometimes writer's block occurs because there are too many distractions around that interrupt your concentration. The distractions may be as elementary as a dripping faucet or the sound of voices upstairs, or more complicated, like worries over other obligations you may have. Whatever the distraction, it's not helping your writing. Try to always devote enough time for writing, and avoid noises or activities that can distract you. If you write with undivided attention, you'll likely finish sooner and have more time to focus on other concerns.

If a tight deadline isn't breathing down your neck, your options for beating writer's block are almost endless. Simply think of something that would relax you and clear out your brain. You can work on a separate project, take a walk, play a video game, watch a movie, read a chapter of a good book, or even take a nap. Some of these stress relievers may be just what you need to unclog your writer's block and let the words flow again.

 Questions

1   What is the purpose of the instructions in this passage?

   A   To amuse readers with stories about students with writer's block
   B   To inform readers about writer's block and ways to reduce its effect
   C   To persuade readers that they have the ability to overcome writer's block
   D   To show readers exactly how to write a story without experiencing writer's block

 Tip

   Go back and skim over the information in the passage. What are these instructions intended to do?

2   What kind of topic does the author suggest that you choose?

   A   a topic that is well known to many people
   B   a topic you've already learned about
   C   a topic that is easy to write about
   D   a topic that interests you

 Tip

   The author suggests that you keep something in mind when choosing a topic. If you don't remember what this was, go back and check the passage.

3   Which of the following is NOT advice given in these instructions?

   A   Taking a nap can relieve stress
   B   Looking at a picture can exercise your brain
   C   Newspaper clippings can give you new ideas
   D   Talking to an older relative can teach you about history

 Tip

   This passage gives many tips on beating writer's block. Read these answer choices carefully. Which of these is not mentioned in the passage?

4   Why does the author include the scenario of the boy staring at the blank page in the beginning of the passage? Use details and information from the passage in your answer.

 # Tip

Think about the author's tone and purpose. Why did he choose to begin his instructions with the short story of the boy?

Now check your answers on the next page.

Passage 3: "Beating Writer's Block"

 **Answers**

1.   B   The article is informative. It tells about writer's block and offers some suggestions for overcoming it. Answer choice B is the best answer.

2.   D   The author suggests that the best topic to work with is one that interests you. That means you'll be excited to write, and your excitement might pass along to the reader.

3.   D   There are many pieces of advice in this passage. However, the author does not mention talking to an older relative. This would be a good idea, but it is not included in the passage.

4.   **Sample answer:** The scenario of the boy in the beginning is one that most of us can relate to, which is why the author includes it in the beginning of the passage. It is an effective lead-in to the hints and instructions that follow.

Passage 4

Now read this passage and answer the questions that follow.

Getting Started with the Guitar

For decades, the guitar has been one of the most popular musical instruments in the world. Millions of people have learned to play the guitar for many different reasons. It can be enjoyable and relaxing to play this instrument, and it's a good form of artistic expression. Some people play by themselves, while others form bands and play for audiences. Whatever your reasons are, the guitar might be just the right instrument for you.

Learning to play the guitar isn't usually very difficult, but it requires dedication. Many people will learn the skills involved rather easily, while others may struggle. Either way, it is necessary for you to have a willingness to learn and practice. The guitar can be a tricky instrument to use. You'll need to learn the skills and then practice them regularly to become a good guitarist.

The first step in learning to play the guitar is finding the right equipment. For a starting guitarist, the following supplies are needed:

Guitar—You won't get far learning the guitar without one! Any functioning guitar should be fine. Perhaps you could even borrow one from a friend or relative, or buy a used one at a yard sale. New guitars can be very expensive. Most beginners don't buy pricey new guitars for themselves until they're certain they are serious about using the instrument.

Guitar pick—A guitar pick is simply a small piece of plastic that you use to pluck the guitar strings. Picks are inexpensive and many people find them easy to misplace, so you may want to get several.

Seat—While playing the guitar, you'll probably want to sit. A stool, or any sort of chair without arms, would be the best choice. It will allow you to place the guitar lengthwise on your lap.

Dedication—You'll need to practice often and learn all you can about playing the guitar. Dedication is essential!

Parts of the Guitar

After you've gathered the necessary equipment, carefully examine your guitar. Although guitars can come in many forms, such as acoustic, electric, and classical, they all share some basic parts. Before you begin playing, it's important to know what these parts of the instrument are for. The diagram below will help you.

The **headstock** is at the top of the guitar. It is a small platform that holds the **tuners**, which are small knobs that you can turn in order to make the strings tighter. By tightening or loosening the strings, you change the sound they make when plucked. Experiment with the tuners by tightening and loosening them, and plucking the strings. You will find that the sound changes a lot. Be careful, though: tightening the strings too much can cause them to snap.

Probably the most important part of the guitar is the **neck**. Located right below the headstock, the neck will likely be the place you'll focus on the most. The neck is divided into sections called **frets**. The strings run down along the frets. If you put your finger on one of the frets, you will change the sound of the strings. Again, try this for yourself. Press your finger onto a fret, and pluck the strings. Then move your finger and try again. You'll quickly find how important the frets are to the sound of the instrument.

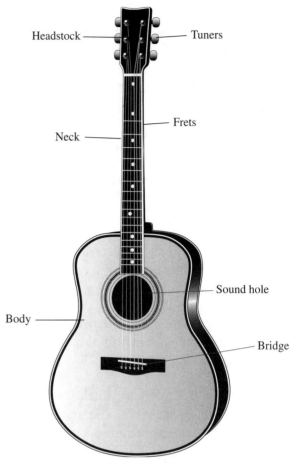

Below the neck is the **body**. This is the largest part of the guitar. You will not have to pay much attention to this part, though. It is basically just a hollow, circular box. In the center is a hole, which catches the sound of the strings and makes it louder. This is called the **sound hole**. Right below the sound hole is the **bridge**, which holds the strings in place.

Holding the Guitar

After you've examined the guitar, it's time to begin figuring out how to play it. Sit on the stool or chair and get comfortable. Then, place the guitar on your lap so that the curve of the guitar body rests on your leg. The instrument should be on its side, with the sound hole facing out. If you are right-handed, you'll probably want the headstock on the left side. If you're left-handed, you'd probably prefer the headstock being on the right.

You should have one hand on the neck of the guitar. This will be your "fret hand" because its main job will be pressing on the frets. Meanwhile, you'll use your "string hand" for plucking the strings near the sound hole.

The Pick

The next thing you need to do is to get a good hold on your guitar pick. Generally, guitar players hold the pick in a special way. To do this, take up a pick in your string hand and make a loose fist with your thumb on top. Then, place the pick under your thumb so that it sticks out slightly. This may feel awkward at first, but you should soon get used to holding the pick like that.

Make Some Noise!

Now, you can finally start making some sounds. Position your "string hand" just over the strings, as close as you can without touching the strings or the body of the guitar. Then, by moving your wrist, use the pick to strike down on one of the strings. Listen carefully to the sound it makes. If the sound buzzes or rattles, you should adjust the tightness of the string. Keep trying until the sound is clear and strong. Then, pluck the other strings, one at a time, and adjust the sounds they make.

Next, do the same thing, but use the pick to strike upwards against the strings. It should sound almost the same as the downward strikes. And finally, try striking down and then up on the same string. This is called *alternate picking*. It may take some practice but it's an important part of playing the guitar.

Getting in Tune

Once you've figured out how to use the pick and make sounds, you want to make sure those sounds are as good as they can be. To ensure this, you should tune your guitar. This is a chore that every guitarist has to do. For the beginner, it can be a tough, even frustrating job, but it gets easier with time and it helps the guitar sound great.

First, you'll need a way to hear the different pitches. This will allow you to test your guitar strings and make sure they match well. You can get "reference pitches" in many ways, including tuning forks, other guitars, or even pianos.

Listen to the reference pitch, and then try the correct string. Keep adjusting the string until it matches the reference pitch. You may have to listen several times. Again, tuning the guitar may take a while at first, but seasoned musicians learn to do it quickly.

Keep Learning

There's almost no end to the guitar skills you can learn once you've mastered these basic skills. The secret is practice, practice, practice. That's where the dedication comes in!

 Questions

1 Why does the author include a diagram of a guitar?

A To help readers see what sort of guitar to buy
B To show readers the parts of the guitar
C To assist readers in handling a guitar
D To compare the sizes of different guitars

 Tip

Look at the diagram carefully. Then look at its location in the instructions. What information is the author trying to give you?

2   What advice does the author give about getting a guitar?

    A   It's important to buy the best guitar you can.

    B   You should only buy a guitar that looks good to you.

    C   Many beginners prefer to use borrowed or inexpensive guitars.

    D   Read books about guitars before you actually purchase one.

 Tip

There is a lot of advice in this passage, but the author only says a few things about getting a guitar. What advice does he give?

3   Which factor may change the way you should hold a guitar?

    A   How tight the guitar strings are

    B   How tall you are

    C   Whether you have an armless chair or a stool

    D   Whether you're left- or right-handed

 Tip

Read over these answer choices carefully. Which might change the way you hold a guitar? If you don't know, look back to the passage for hints.

4   If a second diagram were to be added to the instructions, what would it most likely show?

    A   Methods of tuning a guitar

    B   Places to buy a used guitar

    C   Alternate picking tips

    D   The correct way to hold a pick

 Tip

Think about the skills that are mentioned in the passage. Which of them could be most clarified with a diagram?

5   The author lists several things that are needed to play the guitar well. Which of these things cannot be purchased, and why is it so important? Use information from the passage in your answer.

_____

_____

_____

_____

Tip

Find the list of things needed to play a guitar. You will find one that you can't buy in any store. Why is this one especially important to the guitarist?

Now check your answers on the next page.

Passage 4: "Getting Started with the Guitar"

 Answers

1.　B　The diagram of the guitar is meant to show readers the instrument's major parts. The parts are labeled on the diagram, and each part is described immediately afterwards in the text.

2.　C　The author writes that while all guitarists need a guitar to play, most beginners prefer not to buy an expensive new instrument. More beginners use borrowed or second-hand guitars until they're sure this instrument is right for them.

3.　D　In the section called "Holding the Guitar" the author says that left- and right-handed people usually hold the guitar differently.

4.　D　The first diagram shows the parts of a guitar. A second diagram would probably show the correct way to hold the pick. Holding the pick properly could be tricky. A picture of a hand doing this correctly might be helpful to readers.

5.　　**Sample answer:** One thing that is important for guitar players, but cannot be purchased, is dedication. The author says that it is critical for guitarists to have the dedication to keep practicing what they know, and to continue learning new skills.

Lesson 5: Author's Purpose

Standard 1C: Reading Comprehension

(1.8.24)   **Determine the author's purpose as represented by the choice of genre, and literary devices employed.**

(1.8.25)   **Determine why some points are illustrated.**

Author's Purpose and Design

Most of the questions on the Illinois Standards Achievement Test (ISAT) assessing these skills refer to author's purpose. Authors create pieces of writing for many reasons. They might write a short story to entertain readers or to teach a lesson. They might write an article that gives readers information or teaches them how to do something. Authors sometimes write articles or letters to convince readers to feel as they do or to persuade readers to take a certain action.

Questions about an author's purpose might ask you to identify the purpose of a piece of writing. You might have to decide if a passage is meant to inform, instruct, entertain, or persuade. You might also be asked why an author has chosen to include a certain detail in a passage. To do this, you will have to identify the author's purpose for writing the passage and how including these details might help the author to achieve that purpose.

Activity 1

Determine the author's purpose for each sentence or group of sentences below. Write "entertain," "inform," "teach," or "persuade" in the left-hand column.

Author's Purpose	Sentence
1.	It rained three inches yesterday.
2.	Everyone should recycle unwanted paper.
3.	Once upon a time, there lived a mean old maid named Martha.
4.	Before you begin cleaning your room, you should get rid of all unnecessary clutter.
5.	The author George Eliot was actually a woman writing under a pen name.

Activity 2

In groups of 4 or 5 students, write a convincing advertisement for "Pearly White Toothpaste." Be sure to use persuasive words.

Passage 1

Now read this passage and answer the questions that follow.

Letter to the Principal

Dear Principal Woodbridge,

I am an eighth-grade student at Challenger Junior High School and I belong to the cheerleading squad. As a member of the squad, I practice two nights per week to prepare for the games on Sunday afternoons. During practice, we learn new cheers and routines, make up lines for Sunday's games, and practice building pyramids and perfecting stunts such as back-handsprings, cartwheels, and jumps. I am concerned, however, because several of the girls on our squad also belong to the girls' basketball team and miss practice at least once a week. I am afraid that their failure to make practice will jeopardize the cheerleading squad's overall performance.

It has recently been brought to my attention that the school district may make girls who play basketball and cheer on the cheerleading squad choose between these two extracurricular activities next year. I think this is an excellent idea and I give the school district my full support. Some of the girls who are members of both teams have complained that it's unfair to make them choose between two sports they love equally, but I think it's unfair to their teammates when they miss practices. If everyone else is there putting in the hard work and practice to make the squad better, they should be there, too.

While many people feel that cheerleading is not a real sport, it is a sport in that it takes time, commitment, and hard work to perform well. When girls miss practices for any reason, they miss important strength-training exercises that we use to improve our jumps, our gymnastics, and our pyramid-building skills. They fail to learn the proper techniques for building, which can be dangerous for the other girls on the squad. For example, girls on the squad are divided into two groups: flyers, the girls at the top of the pyramids, and bases, the girls who hold the flyers. When bases miss practice, they fail to learn the appropriate techniques for lifting a girl into the air, holding her steady, and catching her if she falls. When flyers miss practice, they do not get to practice the balance and concentration they need to remain steady while in the air. It's easy to see why missing practice can have disastrous results for the girls on the squad. One slip can cause a whole pyramid to tumble and many girls to get seriously injured.

Another reason why it is important for people attend every practice is because we learn new routines, change old routines, and put together entertaining performances to show off during halftime. Girls who miss practice don't learn the new lines and moves and often lose their place during the halftime show. This makes the whole squad look sloppy and unprepared, which is unfair to the girls on the squad who have perfected the routine by showing up at each and every practice.

I understand that it may be difficult for girls who participate in both sports to choose between them, but I think it's the best thing for both the basketball team and the cheerleading squad. If, however, the

school district decides that the girls should not have to choose, then I think a new practice schedule is in order to end the conflict between basketball practice and cheerleading practice. The school district is responsible for the current practice schedule, so they must revise the schedule to end this conflict.

I propose that the girls' basketball team practice four nights per week, instead of five. This opens one night during the week for cheerleading practice. The other cheerleading practice can be held on Saturday morning or afternoon. In this schedule, the girls that play basketball and cheer would be able to make all of the practices for both teams. While I still feel that the best decision is to make the girls choose between the two sports and dedicate their time to one or the other, a revised schedule is a good alternative.

I would appreciate it if you would bring these concerns and ideas to the attention of the school board so this matter can be resolved as quickly and easily as possible. Thank you for your time and consideration.

Sincerely,

Bhavya Patel

 Questions

1   What is the author's main purpose in writing this letter?

_____

_____

_____

_____

 Tip

Consider the type of information that the author presents in the letter. Why would the author share her opinions with the principal? What is she trying to accomplish with this letter?

2   Why does the author mention an alternate practice schedule?

_____

_____

_____

_____

 Tip

Go back to the passage and reread the part of the letter where the author mentions a revised practice schedule. Why would the author present this idea? What might she accomplish by mentioning an alternate schedule?

3   If a similar problem were taking place at your school, how would you try to solve it? Use information from the passage and your own observations to support your answer.

_____

_____

_____

_____

_____

_____

_____

_____

_____

_____

_____

_____

_____

_____

_____

_____

_____

Tip

Use what you've learned from reading the letter, as well as your own experiences, to answer this question. What would be the best way to try to get this problem solved if it were taking place at your school?

Now check your answers on the next page.

Passage 1: "Letter to the Principal"

 Answers

1. **Sample answer:** The author has written this letter to persuade the principal to make the girls who both cheer and play basketball choose to participate in one sport or the other. She wants to convince him that allowing them to participate in both sports creates a problem that should be solved. The letter is not a story meant to entertain, and it is not an essay written to inform readers about the sport of cheerleading. The letter contains the author's thoughts and opinions, and she is trying to convince the principal that he should agree with her opinions.

2. **Sample answer:** The author mentions an alternate practice schedule to show the principal that if he does not agree with the first solution to the problem, there are other solutions that might also make the situation work for all students involved. Presenting another solution gives the author another chance to convince the principal that her ideas and opinions are good and should be considered. She wants him to bring her ideas to the school board so that this problem can be solved.

3. **Sample answer:** If I had this problem at my school, I would probably also write a letter to the principal, but I think that I would write letters to each member of the school board as well. Since the school board will make the final decision about this problem, they are the people who really need to be persuaded. It might also be a good idea to write a letter to the local newspaper so that the parents of students in sports could think about the issue as well. However, if I could not persuade these parents that making students choose between sports or revising the practice schedule were good ideas, they might make solving the problem more difficult than it already is. I would have to be very confident that my arguments were good enough to convince the majority of parents before I would publish a letter in the newspaper.

Passage 2

Now read this passage and answer the questions that follow.

Cleaning up Keyboard Spills

Most computer users feel perfectly comfortable about working with a beverage beside their keyboard; however, it's all too easy to get whipped up into a working frenzy, wheeling back and forth to different sides of your desk, sorting through stacks of papers and jotting down ideas. Suddenly, your elbow inadvertently nudges your cup, and before you know it, you've got keyboard soup!

Pointless Panic

Many people panic when they've spilled a beverage or other liquid inside of their keyboard, but if you happen to engage in such a mishap—don't be alarmed! While such an accident will certainly terminate your typing for the day, most mistakes such as this are reversible with the appropriate tools and proper knowledge. However, you'll need a whole new set of instructions if you've spilled in a laptop, which is a far more serious situation.

Start the Disassembly

Before you get to cleaning, you need to sever the connection between your keyboard and your computer. Glimpse at the back of your computer tower and find a plug that has a picture of your keyboard, or follow the cord from the keyboard into the tower, and unplug it. Now you are ready to start cleaning.

Diagnose the Disaster

If you have spilled water, you should simply position a towel on the floor or other flat, dryable surface and turn your keyboard upside down on top of the towel, ideally for at least twenty-four hours. This should encourage the water to run out of the keyboard and down into the towel. After this time, flip over the keyboard and let the other side air-dry before plugging it back in. However, if you have spilled something such as soda, juice, or coffee, you will be left with a seriously sticky mess if you don't adhere to the next few steps.

Scouring Stickiness

If you have spilled something sticky, you'll need to remove some of the keys from your keyboard so you can access the inside for thorough cleaning. Before you remove any keys, however, you should sketch the keyboard or take a picture so that you will know where all of the keys belong. Popping a key into the wrong place could be perplexing in the end!

Next, find a flathead screwdriver and carefully pry off the smaller keys, making sure not to put so much pressure on the keys that they crack. You should not pry off the larger keys because they will be much more difficult to remove and replace.

Wet a cotton swab with water and gently swipe all wet and sticky areas on the inside of your keyboard. Let the keyboard dry, and then run a dry cotton swab over the cleaned area. If any of the cotton fuzz sticks to the keyboard, you should clean it again. Stickier messes may call for a little rubbing alcohol on the cotton swab the second time around. If you have spilled something really stubborn, such as orange juice with pulp, you may need to do this several times until it is clean.

Next, wash the removed keys with soap and warm water, then dry them off well with a towel. Let *everything* air-dry for at least twenty-four hours before reassembling your keyboard.

Resume Your Work

Finally, pop your keys back into place and plug in your keyboard. Now you should be primed for typing! If you find that your keys stick when you attempt to type, you'll need to clean it again or take it to a professional. Some spills are bad enough that you may have to purchase a new keyboard, but most can be remedied by following these easy steps.

 Questions

1   Why did the author write this passage?

    A   To show readers different ways that computers can be ruined

    B   To teach readers how to clean a keyboard that has been spilled on

    C   To entertain readers with a funny story about a keyboard spill

    D   To convince readers that they should not keep beverages near their computers

 Tip

Consider the passage type while reading the answer choices. Which choice describes a purpose that is common to this type of passage?

2   Why did the author mention the difference between spilling water and other beverages?

    A   To show that people should only drink water by their computers

    B   To show that other beverages will require more cleaning than water

    C   To show that juice and soda are not as damaging to computers

    D   To show that coffee should never be consumed near a computer

 Tip

    Why would the author want to include this detail? What would it tell the reader about this situation? Reread this part of the passage, and then read the answer choices carefully before choosing the best answer.

3   Why does the author say that most keyboard spills can be remedied by following these easy steps?

    A   She is trying to warn readers that they may have to buy a new keyboard

    B   She wants to let readers know that some steps will not be easy

    C   She is trying to tell readers that these steps will work on any keyboard spill

    D   She wants to reassure readers that keyboards are not expensive items

 Tip

    Go back and reread the passage, paying special attention to the part of the passage in which this point can be found. Why does the author choose to include this detail at this point in the passage?

Now check your answers on the next page.

Passage 2: "Cleaning up Keyboard Spills"

 Answers

1.   B   This passage is a functional, or instructional, passage. Like authors of other instructional passages, the author of "Cleaning up Keyboard Spills" wrote this passage to teach. It does not describe different ways that keyboards can be ruined, and it does not entertain readers with a story about a keyboard spill. The author is not trying to persuade readers; she just wants to teach them.

2.   B   The author mentions the difference between spilling water and other beverages, such as juice, soda, and coffee, on a keyboard to point out to readers that there are more steps involved in cleaning a keyboard on which juice, soda, or coffee has been spilled.

3.   A   The author includes this point because she wants to let readers know that her steps will not work for every keyboard-spill situation. She warns readers that, after following these steps, if their keys are still sticking, they will either have to repeat the steps or purchase another keyboard. She does not guarantee that these steps will fix any keyboard spill.

Passage 3

Chinese Immigration to Angel Island

In the 1800s and 1900s, immigrants flocked to America to escape poverty and oppression and enjoy a better life in "the land of the free." Most of these immigrants were processed, or registered, at an immigration center on Ellis Island in New York City, but those entering the country through California were processed at an immigration center on Angel Island in the San Francisco Bay. Many of these immigrants were from China.

The immigration stations on Ellis and Angel Islands differed in that Angel Island was actually a detention center. While immigrants processed on Ellis Island waited hours or days to enter America, those processed on Angel Island were forced to wait weeks or months. A shortage of jobs in the West and racial prejudice were to blame. A series of discriminatory laws were passed that made it difficult for Asians to enter the United States. The Chinese were the most seriously affected by these laws. More than seventy percent of immigrants detained on Angel Island were Chinese.

Many Chinese initially immigrated to America in search of gold in California, which they nicknamed the "Gold Mountain." They were soon to uncover the fallacy of the "Gold Mountain," however, as they were met with resentment and suspicion from Americans and forced to work menial jobs for little pay. These first immigrants laid railroad tracks, reclaimed swamp land, worked as migrant farmers, and labored in the fishing and mining industries. While they toiled away for long hours under treacherous working conditions, many still remained optimistic about the future and were grateful to be in America, where they were free.

When the American economy faltered in the 1870s, the situation became even more serious for the Chinese. Because the Chinese were willing to work for extremely low wages, Americans living in the West felt that they were the reason for the lack of employment. They passed laws that were even more restrictive, and some Chinese who were already settled in America were cruelly deported to impoverished imperial China. According to these new laws, only persons born in the United States or whose husbands or fathers were U.S. citizens were allowed to enter or remain in the country. Desperate to remain in America, some Chinese managed to falsify "papers" stating that they had fathers who were citizens of the United States. These Chinese were called "paper sons" and "paper daughters." However, this falsification of papers led to an even longer detainment for Chinese trying to enter America—a few were detained for years! They were asked ridiculous questions by interrogators looking for a reason to deport them. Wrote one Chinese detainee:

I told myself that going by this way would be easy.
Who was to know that I would be imprisoned at Devil's Pass?
How was anyone to know that my dwelling place would be a prison?

A new detention center opened on Angel Island in 1910, and its location, which was even more isolated than the first, was considered ideal for interrogations. This new center had space for more detainees and regular boat service to the mainland. Over the next thirty years, 175,000 Chinese immigrants were detained there. To express their feelings of loneliness and fear of brutality and deportation, some detainees carved poetry into the wooden walls of the detention center, some of which is still visible today. Wrote one detainee:

America has power, but not justice.
In prison, we were victimized as if we were guilty.
Given no opportunity to explain, it was really brutal.

Ayala Cove Quarantine Station, Circa 1918

Despite being mistreated, the Chinese permitted to live in America made great contributions to their new country. They supplied labor to American factories, especially during the Civil War when laborers were in short supply. Some Chinese-American entrepreneurs started their own businesses, which sparked the American economy. Using their advanced agricultural knowledge, Chinese-Americans in the West converted what was once useless land into rich farming soil, making the West self-sufficient and no longer dependent upon the East for food. Chinese immigrants brought with them their language, beautiful writing, culture, and customs, which were eventually integrated into American society.

The United States abandoned the detention center on Angel Island in 1940, when "Chinese Exclusion Acts" were repealed and a fire destroyed the administration building. A museum has been established in the old detention center, so visitors can see what life was like for these early Americans. The Angel Island Immigration Station Foundation (AIISF), a non-profit group of concerned individuals and descendants of Chinese-Americans once detained on Angel Island, hopes to preserve and restore the immigration station, which they consider an important part of American history.

 Questions

1   Why does the author quote lines from poetry carved into the walls of the detention center on Angel Island?

A   He wants to show how the Chinese felt about their detainment.

B   He wants to show that the Chinese detained on Angel Island were artistic.

C   He wants to prove that the Chinese on Angel Island were mistreated.

D   He wants to emphasize that the Chinese were there a long time.

 Tip

Go back to the passage and read the parts of the passage that discuss the poetry on the walls. Read these parts as many times as you need to, then look at the answer choices carefully. What was the author discussing when he quoted these lines? What do you think was his purpose for including them in the passage?

2   What was the author's purpose in writing this passage?

A   To entertain readers with a story about Angel Island.

B   To inform readers about a historical event that took place in America.

C   To persuade readers that the detention center workers should be punished.

D   To tell readers why they should not visit the San Francisco Bay.

 Tip

Why would someone write a passage such as this one? Reread the passage. What type of passage is this? What was the author's purpose for writing this passage?

3   Why does the author mention that some Chinese tried to become "paper sons" and "paper daughters"?

  A   To show that some were desperate to stay even though they were treated badly
  B   To show that the Chinese stayed to practice the art of paper folding
  C   To show that many Chinese who came to Angel Island were related to one another
  D   To show that the Chinese would soon become skilled in creating poetry

 Tip

Find the part of the passage where these phrases are discussed and reread this part of the passage. Then read the answer choices carefully. Do not get confused by details in the answer choices, but instead look for the answer choice that explains why the author would include these phrases in this passage.

4   Why do you think the author goes into detail when describing the laws that were passed in America at this time?

_____

_____

_____

_____

 Tip

Why would the author think it was important to include this information in the passage? Read the entire passage again, thinking about this detail as you read. What effect does this information have on the passage? On its readers?

Now check your answers on the next page.

Passage 3: "Chinese Immigration to Angel Island"

 Answers

1. A The author included these lines of poetry because he wanted readers to know how the Chinese felt about their detainment in order to give readers a better understanding of the situation. He wanted to inform readers of more than the historical facts from an outsider's perspective.

2. B The author wrote this passage to inform readers about a historical event. He did not write a fictional story to entertain readers, or an essay or letter to persuade readers that this really happened. He also did not tell readers that they should not visit the San Francisco Bay. His purpose was to teach or to inform.

3. A The author included this detail to show that some Chinese wanted to stay in America even after being imprisoned and treated badly. This information helps readers to understand how these immigrants felt. Some other answer choices describe details from the passage, and one describes a detail that is *not* mentioned in the passage, but answer choice A describes the author's purpose for including this information in the passage.

4.   **Sample answer:** I think that the author included details about these American laws because he wants to inform readers about how bad the situation was for these Chinese immigrants. He wants readers to know that these immigrants had nowhere to turn because there were no laws to protect them.

Passage 4

Now read this passage and answer the questions that follow.

D.C. Dish: A Forum for the Nation

LETTER TO THE EDITOR
New Look for an Old State

To the Editor:

I am writing in response to the many letters that have recently been published addressing the controversy over Georgia's new 2003 state flag. I believe that the new flag is a welcome and necessary change for Georgians, many of whom have been stuck in the past for far too long. While it is encouraging to read letters from individuals supporting and praising alteration of the flag, it is discouraging that some people still think the design of a new flag was unnecessary and that the 2001 flag was a better representation of Georgia as it exists in the United States today.

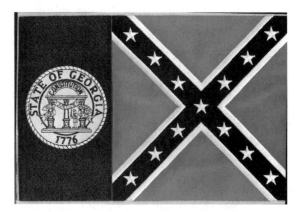

As most citizens of the country are probably aware, the flag adopted by Georgia in 1956 was the subject of heated debate for many years. One-third of this old flag was comprised of the state seal, while the other two-thirds of the flag contained the Confederate Battle Flag, which was carried by Confederate soldiers in the Civil War. Georgia's citizens held mixed feelings about this flag, and the debate divided the state for years. Many African American citizens felt that the Confederate symbol on the flag advocated slavery, racial segregation, and white supremacy, and considered the flag to be an insulting representation of prejudice. Supporters of the flag disputed these claims, stating that the Confederate flag was displayed as a tribute to Confederate soldiers and as a proud symbol of southern history.

Concerns about the prominence of the Confederate flag on the state flag finally prompted then-governor of Georgia, Roy Barnes, to change the state flag in 2001. The 2001 flag contained a large state seal in the middle and a ribbon displaying five different flags that were employed throughout the history of the state and the country, one of which was the questionable flag that was being replaced. Georgians found themselves in an uproar once again. Those who supported the old flag were outraged that the Confederate symbol appeared to be small and insignificant, while those who objected to

the old flag could not understand why the offensive Confederate symbol was still displayed. In a passionate speech to Georgia's citizens, Governor Barnes urged the people of the state to accept the new flag, assuring them that it both represented the unity of Georgia's people and embraced the state's heritage at the same time. The people begged for the right to vote on the new flag, and so began a lengthy and difficult legal process, during which Governor Barnes was voted out of office.

I think that the fight to incorporate the Confederate flag into the new Georgia state flag was invalid and insulting to African American citizens, not only of Georgia, but of the United States in general. While many argue that the Confederate flag is a tribute to Confederate soldiers, are Americans truly expected to believe that the flag is not a tribute to and representation of the days when African Americans were not even considered citizens and had no rights or powers?

I don't really understand why Georgians feel the need to display a representation of the Confederacy on their flag in the first place. A state flag should represent a state as a whole, not a snapshot of the country's history in which a state participated. Perhaps I might better understand the desire to hold on to this symbol if I were actually from Georgia. Yet being from the District of Columbia, a northern state, I can tell you that as an outsider watching this debate, this fight for the Confederate flag does not reflect well on Georgia as a whole, and is probably causing the rest of the country to view Georgian citizens as stubborn and resistant to change. While this view may reflect some Georgian citizens, it certainly cannot speak for all people living in Georgia. I feel for those Georgian citizens who want to progress with the rest of the country and are being held back by those who want to live in the past. Georgia has historically always been behind the rest of the country — it was even the last of the thirteen colonies to be founded, having been created fifty years after the twelfth colony, Pennsylvania. Though this pattern continues, I think that Georgians should work to change their slow progression and give the state a new reputation, allow it to fast forward into the future rather than pause in the past.

Georgia's history is rich and interesting, and while the days of the Civil War will never be forgotten or diminished in importance, Georgia's citizens must learn to move forward and embrace the mix of people that currently makes up the state's citizenship, just as the former Confederate-flag-waving states of Alabama and South Carolina have done. Governor Barnes' attempt to encourage citizens to define their shared identity by present standards rather than those of the past was progressive and admirable, and I was shocked and dismayed at the number of people who were unwilling to do so. While it is common to fear change, communities — both large and small — must change in some ways because this is the nature of the world and of life, the more obstinate people are in resisting such change, the more slowly the state, and the country as a whole, will develop. Barnes was not trying to take away Georgia's history or pride, he was trying to replace a symbol of hate and turmoil with a new symbol of unity and peace, one that more accurately represents the evolution of the state and country over the many years that have passed since the days of the Civil War.

Georgian citizens are not prohibited from displaying the Confederate flag in their homes, on their clothing, or on their vehicles. Individual freedom of expression is a right guaranteed by the First Amendment of the U. S. Constitution, and this freedom was not abused during the adoption of a new state flag. The Georgia flag — as any state flag — does not represent individuals, it represents a state, and Georgian lawmakers decided that since the Confederate flag was a symbol that was representative of only a portion of the state's citizens (and offensive to another portion), it should be replaced. I think this was an excellent decision.

The 2001 flag has been replaced with a new flag, one that contains no images or representations of the Confederate flag. While the 2003 flag is neutral and not directly offensive to any one group of people, the intensity and duration of the fight to keep the Confederate flag was discouraging. Just when it seemed that the country has moved leaps and bounds away from hate and discrimination, up popped another reminder that we still have such a long way to go. We need to learn to embrace history while at the same time progressing toward better ideals and situations. We need to remember the hardships of the past, learn from them, and move forward. Citizens of Georgia and of the United States, let us move forward together, away from hate, away from the pain of history and war, and toward a more accepting and tolerant future. After all, our differences are a large part of what makes America such a wonderful and unique place to live.

Sincerely,

Reginald Furor
Washington, DC

 Questions

1   Why does the author mention Georgia's place in colonial history?

A   To show that Georgia did not have an important role in the Civil War
B   To show that Georgia has offended other states since its beginning
C   To show that Georgia has always been behind the rest of the country
D   To show that Georgia had a slow start but is now developing quickly

 Tip

Go back and reread the part of the passage that mentions the thirteen colonies. Why does the author choose to include this information?

2   Why did the author write this letter?

A   To persuade readers that changing the Georgia flag was a good idea
B   To entertain readers with a personal story about the Georgia flag
C   To explain to readers why the Georgia flag was originally changed
D   To inform readers of some interesting elements in Georgia history

Tip

Consider the contents of the letter. What does the author discuss in the letter? Why would the author want to make these points?

3   What is the author's purpose in discussing the First Amendment?

A   To show that it doesn't matter if some people are offended by the flag
B   To discuss ways in which Georgians have broken the law
C   To prove that the use of the Confederate flag in this way is wrong
D   To show that Georgians can display the Confederate flag in personal ways

Tip

Find the part of the passage in which the author mentions the First Amendment. Then read each answer choice carefully. What is the author's purpose in mentioning the First Amendment?

4   What is the purpose of writing a letter such as this one and sending it to a newspaper? Use information from the passage and your own observations to support your answer.

_____

_____

_____

_____

Tip

This question asks you what purpose is served by a letter to the editor. Have you ever read a letter like this in a newspaper? Why would someone want others to read this type of letter?

Now check your answers on the next page.

Passage 4: "Letter to the Editor: New Look for an Old State"

 Answers

1. C The author mentions colonial history to show that Georgia has always been slower to develop than the rest of the country. The other answer choices describe opinions that were not expressed by the author and therefore could not reflect the author's purpose. Answer choice C is the best answer.

2. A The purpose of this letter is to persuade the readers to accept the author's opinion that Georgians should more forward and let go of their old flag. It is not an informative essay or an entertaining story. The letter was not written to explain why the flag was changed, but to persuade readers to believe that it was a good idea to change it.

3. D The author mentions the First Amendment when he is discussing alternative ways for Georgians to express their historical pride by displaying the Confederate flag in a personal manner rather than on the state flag. Therefore, answer choice D is the best answer.

4.   **Sample answer:** Editorial letters are written to express a person's opinion. However, I think the purpose of expressing one's opinion in this way is to convince others to share the opinion. Publishing an editorial letter in a newspaper is a great way to share an opinion with hundreds, thousands, or even millions of people. I think that people send these letters for publication because they know that it is a great way to try to convince many people at once that their opinion is correct and that those who read the letter should share that opinion. It is also an easier way to convince or persuade people to believe something than a two-sided debate because if readers want to hear the other side of the story, they have to create disputing arguments for themselves. While people often read an editorial letter and then send a disputing letter, these letters are not printed until the first letter has already been seen by the public and therefore, the original author may have already convinced people that his or her ideas are correct or desirable.

Lesson 6: Drawing Conclusions and Making Inferences

Standard 1C: Reading Comprehension

(1.8.14)   Determine the answer to a literal or simple inference question regarding the meaning of a passage.

(1.8.19)   Draw inferences, conclusions, or generalizations about text and support them with textual evidence and prior knowledge.

(1.8.20)   Differentiate between conclusions that are based on fact and those that are based on opinion.

(1.8.21)   Explain information presented in a nonfiction passage using evidence from the passage.

(1.8.22)   Use information from a variety of sources to explain a situation or decision or to solve a problem.

What are conclusions and inferences?

When you draw a conclusion or make an inference, you draw personal meaning from a passage. These types of questions are not stated in the passage, so you won't be able to put your finger on them. You have to determine the answer based on what you have read. In other words, you have to think carefully about what you have read.

When you draw a conclusion, you make a judgment or form an opinion based on what you read or what you already know. When you make an inference, you often predict something that will happen based on the facts at hand. You might surmise or guess something about a person, idea, or thing. For example, suppose you are a reading a mystery novel. You are about half-way through it when you conclude that the maid did it, but you also infer that she is crafty and will try to frame the butler.

On the ISAT, questions asking you to draw a conclusion or make an inference often begin with "why" or "how" and/or include the words "probably" or "most likely."

Activity

Look at the picture above. Draw a conclusion about the two men. Make an inference about what they will do next. Share your conclusion and prediction with the class.

_____

_____

_____

_____

_____

_____

Passage 1

Now read this passage and answer the questions that follow.

Excerpt from *War of the Worlds*
by H.G. Wells

CHAPTER ONE—THE EVE OF THE WAR

No one would have believed in the last years of the nineteenth century that this world was being watched keenly and closely by intelligences greater than man's and yet as mortal as his own; that as men busied themselves about their various concerns they were scrutinised and studied, perhaps almost as narrowly as a man with a microscope might scrutinise the transient creatures that swarm and multiply in a drop of water. With infinite complacency men went to and fro over this globe about their little affairs, serene in their assurance of their empire over matter. It is possible that the infusoria under the microscope do the same. No one gave a thought to the older worlds of space as sources of human danger, or thought of them only to dismiss the idea of life upon them as impossible or improbable. It is curious to recall some of the mental habits of those departed days. At most terrestrial men fancied there might be other men upon Mars, perhaps inferior to themselves and ready to welcome a missionary enterprise. Yet across the gulf of space, minds that are to our minds as ours are to those of the beasts that perish, intellects vast and cool and unsympathetic, regarded this earth with envious eyes, and slowly and surely drew their plans against us. And early in the twentieth century came the great disillusionment.

The planet Mars, I scarcely need remind the reader, revolves about the sun at a mean distance of 140,000,000 miles, and the light and heat it receives from the sun is barely half of that received by this world. It must be, if the nebular hypothesis has any truth, older than our world; and long before this earth ceased to be molten, life upon its surface must have begun its course. The fact that it is scarcely one seventh of the volume of the earth must have accelerated its cooling to the temperature at which life could begin. It has air and water and all that is necessary for the support of animated existence.

Yet so vain is man, and so blinded by his vanity, that no writer, up to the very end of the nineteenth century, expressed any idea that intelligent life might have developed there far, or indeed at all, beyond its earthly level. Nor was it generally understood that since Mars is older than our earth, with scarcely a quarter of the superficial area and remoter from the sun, it necessarily follows that it is not only more distant from time's beginning but nearer its end.

The secular cooling that must someday overtake our planet has already gone far indeed with our neighbour. Its physical condition is still largely a mystery, but we know now that even in its equatorial region the midday temperature barely approaches that of our coldest winter. Its air is much more attenuated than ours, its oceans have shrunk until they cover but a third of its surface, and as its slow seasons change huge snowcaps gather and melt about either pole and periodically inundate its temperate zones. That last stage of exhaustion, which to us is still incredibly remote, has become a present-day problem for the inhabitants of Mars. The immediate pressure of necessity has brightened their intellects, enlarged their powers, and hardened their hearts. And looking across space with instruments, and intelligences such as we have scarcely dreamed of, they see, at its nearest distance only 35,000,000 of miles sunward of them, a morning star of hope, our own warmer planet, green with vegetation and grey with water, with a cloudy atmosphere eloquent of fertility, with glimpses through its drifting cloud wisps of broad stretches of populous country and narrow, navy-crowded seas.

And we men, the creatures who inhabit this earth, must be to them at least as alien and lowly as are the monkeys and lemurs to us. The intellectual side of man already admits that life is an incessant struggle for existence, and it would seem that this too is the belief of the minds upon Mars. Their world is far gone in its cooling and this world is still crowded with life, but crowded only with what they regard as inferior animals. To carry warfare sunward is, indeed, their only escape from the destruction that, generation after generation, creeps upon them.

And before we judge of them too harshly we must remember what ruthless and utter destruction our own species has wrought, not only upon animals, such as the vanished bison and the dodo, but upon its inferior races. The Tasmanians, in spite of their human likeness, were entirely swept out of existence in a war of extermination waged by European immigrants, in the space of fifty years. Are we such apostles of mercy as to complain if the Martians warred in the same spirit?

The Martians seem to have calculated their descent with amazing subtlety—their mathematical learning is evidently far in excess of ours—and to have carried out their preparations with a well-nigh perfect unanimity. Had our instruments permitted it, we might have seen the gathering trouble far back in the nineteenth century. Men like Schiaparelli watched the red planet—it is odd, by-the-bye, that for countless centuries Mars has been the star of war—but failed to interpret the fluctuating appearances of the markings they mapped so well. All that time the Martians must have been getting ready.

 Questions

1   Why does the narrator state that planet Earth must look like a morning star of hope to the Martians?

   A   Because the Martians want humans to teach them how to build advanced instruments
   B   Because the Martians are wearing out their planet and will need to take over Earth
   C   Because planet Earth is bright and it is 35,000,000 miles away from Mars
   D   Because planet Earth's creatures are superior and can help the Martians progress

 Tip

Go back and read this part of the passage. What is the author discussing? What can you conclude from this statement?

2   According to the passage, why weren't humans prepared for the Martian invasion?

   A   Humans didn't know that the planet Mars existed.
   B   Humans didn't have the right weapons to fight the Martian invaders.
   C   Humans didn't think there was intelligent life on other planets.
   D   Humans didn't have spaceships to fight off Martians.

 Tip

Think about what the narrator said about mankind in the beginning of this passage. How might this make humans unprepared for a Martian invasion?

3   Why does the narrator feel that humans are destructive?

A   We have wiped out both animal and human life.

B   We have not been friendly with the Martians in the past.

C   We have used up all of our clean air and water.

D   We have not been aware that we are being watched.

 ## Tip

Near the end of the passage, the narrator states that humans should not judge the Martians too harshly because humans are destructive. Why does the narrator feel this way?

Now check your answers on the next page.

Passage 1: "Excerpt from *War of the Worlds*"

 Answers

1. B The author states that because Mars is older than planet Earth, it is experiencing environmental problems that planet Earth has not yet had to deal with. Planet Earth gives the Martians hope because they know that when they finally wear out their own planet, they can take over Earth and live there.

2. C The passage tells the reader that the reason humans weren't prepare was because they thought that we were the only intelligent life forms in the universe. Therefore, the correct answer is choice C.

3. A In the sixth paragraph of this passage, the narrator points out that humans should not judge the Martians' destructive actions because we have also wiped out species of animals and races of people.

Passage 2

Now read this passage and answer the questions that follow.

How to Make an Origami Sailboat

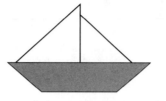

Origami is the art of paper folding. The origin of the art has been debated by scholars for ages. Some scholars believe that origami was developed in China, while others claim that it was invented by the Japanese. Regardless of its origin, origami is a tradition that has been around for hundreds of years, delighting people with simple and beautiful pieces of art. While folding paper might not seem very interesting at first, people who practice origami can turn an ordinary piece of paper into anything from an elegant swan to realistic paper roses. That's pretty amazing!

One of the best things about this hobby is its simplicity. The only materials you need are a piece of paper and your own two hands. You can also practice anywhere you can find a flat surface. If you're interested, it's time to give origami a try!

The following instructions will show you how to make an easy paper sailboat. Grab a piece of paper and carefully follow these directions.

Step 1: Find yourself a perfectly square piece of paper. Though you can buy paper made specifically for origami, you don't have to rush out to the store to do this activity. You can cut any ordinary piece of paper into a square to use in the following steps.

Step 2: Start with one of the four points of the paper facing towards you. Fold the bottom point to meet the top point so that it makes a crease. Unfold the paper. Repeat this step with the point on the right, folding it so that it meets the point on the left and makes a crease. Once you have finished, unfold the paper.

Step 3: Turn the paper so that one of the edges faces you. Fold the bottom edge to the top edge and make a crease. Unfold. Repeat this step by folding the right edge to the left edge and make a crease. Unfold the paper and turn it so that a point is facing you again.

Step 4: Take hold of the right and left points and fold them into the middle so that they meet at the bottom point and flatten. This should give you a diamond-shaped piece of paper.

Step 5: Take hold of the bottom point and fold it up to the right so that the crease you make follows the line where the folds of the right and the left sides of the diamond meet.

Step 6: Turn the paper over.

Step 7: Fold the very bottom corner of the paper up to the base and crease. Unfold slightly so that it makes a little stand. This will help your boat stand upright.

Congratulations! You have just finished your first piece of origami! This is just one of the variations of a sailboat that you can make using origami. Some of the others are quite elaborate and difficult. However, if you are interested in learning more about origami you can find some great books on the subject at your local library or bookstore. With enough practice and patience, anyone can learn how to make even the most intricate origami figures.

 Questions

1   According to the author, what materials are required for origami?

A   Scissors, paper, and tape
B   Sheets of colored paper and a book about origami
C   Two hands and a piece of paper
D   Special origami paper and a flat surface

 Tip

Find the part of the passage where the author discusses the necessary materials for origami and reread the paragraph. Which materials are required?

2   Which step from the passage calls for you to begin folding?

A   Step 1
B   Step 2
C   Step 4
D   Step 7

 Tip

Look at the steps listed in the passage and find the step where folding is first mentioned.

3 Which statement from the passage is an opinion?

A "The origin of the art has been debated by scholars for ages."
B "This is just one of the variations of a sailboat that you can make using origami."
C "One of the best things about this hobby is its simplicity."
D "Origami is the art of paper folding."

 Tip

Read these sentences and think about what it is that makes a statement an opinion. Which of these sentences has the characteristics of an opinion?

4 The author mentions the library and bookstore as sources of more information about origami. Where else might you find out more about origami?

A In a Chinese cookbook
B On the Internet
C In a fashion magazine
D On the back of a notebook

 Tip

Look at the choices and eliminate the ones you know will not contain any information about origami. You should be able to pick the correct answer after eliminating all of the obvious wrong answers.

Now check your answers on the next page.

Passage 2: "How to Make an Origami Sailboat"

 Answers

1. C   In paragraph three, the author mentions that the only materials you need to engage in origami are a piece of paper and your own two hands. While a flat surface and special origami paper are mentioned, they are not required materials.

2. B   The author instructs readers to begin folding in Step 2. The correct answer is B.

3. C   The author holds the opinion that one of the best things about origami is its simplicity. This statement cannot be proven. Answer choice C is the best answer.

4. B   After thinking about each of the answer choices, you should be able to tell that answer choices A, C, and D would not contain information about origami. You probably know that it is easy to find information about most topics on the Internet, and that the Internet most likely contains information about origami as well.

Passage 3

Now read this passage and answer the questions that follow.

Excerpt from *Dracula*
by Bram Stoker

MINA HARKER'S JOURNAL

29 September.—After I had tidied myself, I went down to Dr. Seward's study. At the door I paused a moment, for I thought I heard him talking with some one. As, however, he had pressed me to be quick, I knocked at the door, and on his calling out, "Come in," I entered.

To my intense surprise, there was no one with him. He was quite alone, and on the table opposite him was what I knew at once from the description to be a phonograph. I had never seen one, and was much interested.

"I hope I did not keep you waiting," I said, "but I stayed at the door as I heard you talking, and thought there was someone with you."

"Oh," he replied with a smile, "I was only entering my diary."

"Your diary?" I asked him in surprise.

"Yes," he answered. "I keep it in this." As he spoke he laid his hand on the phonograph.

I felt quite excited over it, and blurted out, "Why, this beats even shorthand! May I hear it say something?"

"Certainly," he replied with alacrity, and stood up to put it in train for speaking. Then he paused, and a troubled look overspread his face.

"The fact is," he began awkwardly, "I only keep my diary in it, and as it is entirely, almost entirely, about my cases it may be awkward, that is, I mean . . ." He stopped, and I tried to help him out of his embarrassment.

"You helped to attend dear Lucy at the end. Let me hear how she died, for all that I know of her, I shall be very grateful. She was very, very dear to me."

To my surprise, he answered, with a horrorstruck look in his face, "Tell you of her death? Not for the wide world!"

"Why not?" I asked, for some grave, terrible feeling was coming over me.

Again he paused, and I could see that he was trying to invent an excuse. At length, he stammered out, "You see, I do not know how to pick out any particular part of the diary."

Even while he was speaking an idea dawned upon him, and he said with unconscious simplicity, in a different voice, and with the naiveté of a child, "That's quite true, upon my honour."

I could not but smile, at which he grimaced. "I gave myself away that time!" he said. "But do you know that, although I have kept the diary for months past, it never once struck me how I was going to find any particular part of it in case I wanted to look it up?"

By this time my mind was made up that the diary of a doctor who attended Lucy might have something to add to the sum of our knowledge of that terrible Being, and I said boldly, "Then, Dr. Seward, you had better let me copy it out for you on my typewriter."

He grew to a positively deathly pallor as he said, "No! No! No! For all the world. I wouldn't let you know that terrible story!"

Then it was terrible. My intuition was right! For a moment, I thought, and as my eyes ranged the room, unconsciously looking for something or some opportunity to aid me, they lit on a great batch of typewriting on the table. His eyes caught the look in mine, and without his thinking, followed their direction. As they saw the parcel he realized my meaning.

"You do not know me," I said. "When you have read those papers, my own diary and my husband's also, which I have typed, you will know me better. I have not faltered in giving every thought of my own heart in this cause. But, of course, you do not know me, yet, and I must not expect you to trust me so far."

He is certainly a man of noble nature. Poor dear Lucy was right about him. He stood up and opened a large drawer, in which were arranged in order a number of hollow cylinders of metal covered with dark wax, and said, "You are quite right. I did not trust you because I did not know you. But I know you now, and let me say that I should have known you long ago. I know that Lucy told you of me. She told me of you too. May I make the only atonement in my power? Take the cylinders and hear them. The first half-dozen of them are personal to me, and they will not horrify you. Then you will know me better. Dinner will by then be ready. In the meantime I shall read over some of these documents, and shall be better able to understand certain things."

He carried the phonograph himself up to my sitting room and adjusted it for me. Now I shall learn something pleasant, I am sure. For it will tell me the other side of a true love episode of which I know one side already.

 Questions

1   What do Mina and Dr. Seward have in common?

    A   They are both doctors.
    B   They are both married.
    C   They both knew Lucy.
    D   They are both writers.

 Tip

Mina and Dr. Seward do not know each other very well, but they have one connection. Think about this as you read through the answer choices.

2   What is it that Dr. Seward doesn't want Mina to hear?

    A   the story of how Lucy died
    B   his personal feelings for Lucy
    C   the story of his own life
    D   his fear of Dracula

 Tip

Mina specifically asks to hear something from Dr. Seward's diary. Think about what that is and then choose your answer.

3   Which of the following items is most like a phonograph?

    A   A computer
    B   A telephone
    C   A television
    D   A tape recorder

 Tip

Think about what Dr. Seward uses the phonograph for and pick the item that does the same thing.

4   Why does Dr. Seward say that he has given himself away?

A   He says that his statement is true, which lets Mina know that he intended to lie.

B   He pretends not to be upset about Lucy's death, but Mina knows that he is sad.

C   He says that he does not know Mina, which lets Mina know that he has already read her diary.

D   He pretends to be alone in the room, but Mina knows that he was speaking to someone.

 Tip

Reread the part of the story in which Dr. Seward says that he has given himself away. Why does he say this? To what is he referring?

Now check your answers on the next page.

Passage 3: "Excerpt from *Dracula*"

 Answers

1.　C　Lucy is the only connection between Mina and Dr. Seward. Mina is not a doctor and Seward is neither married nor a writer. Therefore, the correct answer is C.

2.　A　Dr. Seward says he wants to keep Mina from hearing the terrible details of Lucy's death. Therefore, the correct answer is A.

3.　D　Dr. Seward uses the phonograph to record his voice. A tape recorder performs the same function. Answer choice D is correct.

4.　A　Dr. Seward tries to lie to Mina so she will not keep asking him to hear about Lucy's death, but he realizes that his lie is actually true. Choice A is the best answer.

Passage 4

Now read this passage and answer the questions that follow.

William Wallace and the Fight for Scotland

Around seven hundred years ago, Scotland began fighting for its freedom from England. The meadows of Scotland became the scenes of many bloody battles, and from these battles, William Wallace rose to fame. Wallace, a Scottish leader, inspired great fear among his enemies and wild enthusiasm among his allies. Hundreds of tales, both fact and fiction, followed Wallace's accomplishments. Today, the historical truth behind his amazing story can be difficult to find.

Most historians agree that Wallace was born around 1270 near Ayrshire, Scotland. He most likely spent his early years living with an uncle. His uncle was a priest, and taught Wallace about religion. Wallace rounded out his education with physical training in martial arts like swordsmanship and horsemanship.

Wallace grew into a large, imposing man, thought to be over six and a half feet tall—about eighteen inches taller than the average man at the time! Wallace was also known to be handsome, charming, and thoughtful to the needs of his neighbors. While Wallace studied, trained, and developed his abilities, however, his beloved Scotland began to face one crisis after another.

The king of Scotland, Alexander III, had guided the country through two decades of peace and prosperity. Most importantly, he had protected its independence from England, which claimed the power to control many of Scotland's decisions. In 1286, Alexander III died during a fierce storm. Since Alexander III had no heirs, his granddaughter Margaret was declared queen of Scotland. Margaret was only four years old at the time, and she lived in Norway!

This situation caused concern and confusion among the nobles of Scotland. It was also noticed by King Edward I of England. King Edward, known as Edward Longshanks, used the confusion in Scotland to increase England's control over it. When young Margaret died of illness in 1290, Edward Longshanks put a new plan into effect.

While Scottish nobles schemed and fought for power, Longshanks moved English armies into Scotland. These armies built forts and stockades. They quickly became known for abusing the people of Scotland. It seemed that nobody could stop them. Then, once again, the situation worsened for the Scots. Longshanks used his influence to bring a new king into power. When that king failed to obey English rules, Longshanks launched a bloody invasion of Scotland. In five months, Edward Longshanks conquered Scotland and set up English rulers and laws all around the country.

The Scots proved to have a very strong sense of independence and national pride. They did not want to be controlled. They resented the presence of English soldiers in their country. The soldiers continued to abuse the Scottish people, making them more and more angry. It was only a matter of time before war broke out again.

When William Wallace's father was killed by English soldiers, Wallace became determined to force the invaders out of Scotland. He began leading a ragtag group of Scottish warriors against the English soldiers. In one of his first battles, he was captured and imprisoned in a dungeon without food or medicine. Some local people rescued him and nursed him back to health.

With his health restored, Wallace found even more strength for fighting the English. He drafted more angry Scottish peasants into his army and began attacking the English troops. According to legend, Wallace even hunted down and defeated the knight who had killed his father. By 1297, Wallace and his friend, Sir Andrew de Moray, launched a number of attacks on English forts. Surprised by their successes in battle, they next focused on their greatest challenge of all: Stirling Castle.

A large English army was camped in Stirling Castle, located near Wallace's uncle's home. Wallace knew the area very well and used his knowledge wisely. Leaders of the English army predicted that Wallace and de Moray would retreat at the first sign of danger. When the English marched an army toward Wallace's group of peasant warriors, they expected the Scots to panic and run away.

Instead, Wallace led his small army to a nearby bridge and attacked the English troops as they crossed it. Thousands of English soldiers were killed in the fight. Wallace proved that the Scottish were able to fight back against the English. He and de Moray marched bravely forward and captured Stirling Castle.

William Wallace immediately became a beloved hero among the Scottish peasants. They gathered around him, looking for guidance and helping to support his missions against the English invaders. The peasants began to hope he could be their greatest hero and could win back Scotland's freedom. Wallace was even made a knight and declared the guardian of Scotland in 1297. However, Scottish leaders and nobles were not as pleased as the peasants were. They preferred to go along with the demands of the English and cooperate with Edward Longshanks. They did not have much faith in Wallace's heroic acts and abilities, no matter how impressive they seemed.

Their hesitation to support Wallace seemed justified in 1298, when Edward Longshanks led a gigantic English army into Scotland to defeat Wallace once and for all. Using thousands of archers armed with bows and arrows, Longshanks battered Wallace's army. Historians believe that nearly ten thousand Scots may have died in that battle.

After the defeat, Wallace fled into the forests. He left his military command to Robert de Bruce and Sir John Comyn. Wallace spent years fleeing from Longshanks's soldiers, until finally he was captured in 1305. Although most Scots saw Wallace as a national hero, the English called him a traitor. He was executed on August 23, 1305.

His death was not at all in vain, however. In William Wallace, the Scots had found a timeless hero. News of his death angered the Scottish people so much that they began a new rebellion to win independence. Within a year, the country had broken free from England, and Robert de Bruce was crowned king of Scotland.

To this day, people continue to be fascinated by the story of William Wallace. The facts of his life are sketchy at times, largely because of the strong feelings he caused in those around him. Many Scots loved him and viewed him as the greatest national hero of all time. At the same time, many English people disliked and feared Wallace, and told stories of his uncivilized actions.

Despite this, there is no question that William Wallace was a brave Scottish patriot. He fought against the oppression of his country, both by the English and by crooked Scottish nobles. He gave his life to help his people become free.

 **Questions**

1   What probably makes it the most difficult to find true historical accounts of William Wallace's life?

    A   Wallace was captured by the English army before he could create a record of his accomplishments.

    B   Wallace's acts of heroism led people to tell both factual and fictional stories about his achievements.

    C   Scottish nobles did not like Wallace and told false stories about him to discredit his skill and bravery in battle.

    D   Wallace and his army suffered a few crushing defeats that caused people to lose faith in his abilities.

 Tip

Read the first few and last few paragraphs of the passage. What does the author say about William Wallace?

2   Which of the following most likely helped Wallace defeat the English army at Stirling Castle?

    A   He grew up near the castle and knew the area well.

    B   He was handsome, charming, and thoughtful to his neighbors.

    C   He was determined to avenge his father's death.

    D   He launched a surprise attack on the English army.

 Tip

Read the paragraphs about the attack on Stirling Castle. What benefit did Wallace have that the English army did not?

3   Which of the following shows that William Wallace was brave and selfless?

    A   Wallace wanted to find and defeat the knight who had killed his father.

    B   Wallace was a hero to the Scottish people but a traitor to the English.

    C   Wallace died trying to help the Scottish people maintain their freedom.

    D   Wallace fled into the forest to escape being captured by the English army.

 Tip

Recall the events surrounding Wallace's rise to fame and how he eventually died. Why was Wallace viewed as a hero?

Now check your answers on the next page.

Passage 4: "William Wallace and the Fight for Scotland"

 Answers

1. B   In the first few and last few paragraphs, the author explains that Wallace's heroic actions caused the Scottish people to tell both factual and fictional stories about his accomplishments. In addition, the passage says that the English people spread stories that Wallace was uncivilized. Answer choice B is the best answer.

2. A   According to the passage, Wallace grew up in his uncle's home right near Stirling Castle. He used his knowledge of the area to aid in his attack on the English troops. He led his army to a nearby bridge where they were able to defeat much of the English army. Answer choice A is the best answer.

3. C   Wallace became a hero to the Scottish people by fighting to keep English control out of Scotland. Eventually, the English army captured and killed Wallace. He died trying to help the Scottish people keep their independence. Answer choice C is the best answer.

Lesson 7: Understanding Literature

Standard 2A: Literary Elements and Techniques

(2.8.01)   Identify elements of fiction: theme, rising action, falling action, conflict, point of view, resolution, and flashback.

(2.8.02)   Explain how theme, rising action, falling action, conflict, point of view, and resolution contribute to the meaning and a reader's interpretation of a literary selection.

(2.8.03)   Identify the author's message or theme.

(2.8.04)   Compare stories to personal experience, prior knowledge, or other stories

(2.8.05)   Recognize points of view in narratives. (e.g., first person).

(2.8.06)   Determine what characters are like by their words, thoughts, and actions, as well as how other characters react to them.

(2.8.07)   Determine character motivation.

(2.8.08)   Identify conflict or contradiction within a character or a character's behavior.

(2.8.09)   Explain the relationship between main and supporting characters.

(2.8.10)   Identify literary devices: (e.g., figurative language, hyperbole, understatement, symbols, dialogue).

(2.8.11)   Explain how the literary devices (e.g., imagery, metaphor, figurative language dialogue) contribute to the meaning of a literary selection.

(2.8.12)   Identify varieties of irony, including dramatic irony.

Standard 2B: Variety of Literary Works

(2.8.13)   Identify various subcategories of genres: poetry, drama (comedy and tragedy), science fiction, historical fiction, myth or legend, biography/autobiography, story, poem, fairy tale, folktale, fable, nonfiction, and essay.

Literature Questions

Literature is more than just groups of words. There are many elements and techniques involved in literature. To get a full grasp on the literature, readers need to learn how to identify, understand, and use these elements and techniques.

ISAT questions dealing with literary elements and techniques may ask you to analyze the characters in a story. Who are they, and what are their behaviors, personalities, and motivations? Questions might ask you to identify parts of the story, including theme, flashback, conflict, and resolution. Questions about literary devices (such as figurative language, imagery, and dialogue) and about genres of literature (like fiction, nonfiction, myth, and science fiction) will also likely be asked on the ISAT.

 **Activity**

In a sentence or two, summarize the plot of a story that matches each of the literary genres below. It can be a story you've read or one you made up. The first has been done for you.

Literary Genre:	Example Plot:
1. Myth	A cursed king turns everything he touches into gold.
2. Comedy	
3. Tragedy	
4. Historical fiction	
5. Science fiction	
6. Biography	

Passage 1

Now read this passage and answer the questions that follow.

New Problems for New Jake

Jake recalled being happy when he was a little boy. When he'd toddled around his parents' legs, or spent entire afternoons with his imagination and action figures, he felt secure and loved. Now, Jake was an adolescent, with a constant abundance of schoolwork, greasy skin, and the feeling that everything he did was wrong. He used to be boisterous and joyful, and now he just tried to be quiet. Whenever he said anything, he always seemed to embarrass himself.

More than anything, Jake envied the more popular kids in his class. He watched them every day laughing and socializing. They had all the newest clothes, the best haircuts, and the most friends. It occurred to Jake that they had all the benefits and he had all the burdens. After a while, he decided that the best thing he could do to improve himself would be to become one of the popular kids.

Jake decided to reinvent his entire image. He gathered all of his birthday money and his lawn-mowing money, and went into town. Over the next few hours he bankrupted himself, but when he returned home, he looked like a whole new Jake. He had fancy clothes and a trendy haircut. He was eager to go to school the next day and assume his position among the popular kids.

When he got to school, he surprised many people with his new look. Some of the students seemed to notice him for the first time. However, their reactions weren't as positive as he had hoped they would be. Most of the kids seemed to view him with curiosity or confusion, rather than with admiration. Nobody raced up to Jake, complimenting him or asking to be his friend.

The popular kids in his classes did not flock to him, either. A few muttered to one another, "Is that the same Jake who used to sit in the corner?" They agreed it was the same Jake, but he looked different. Then, they ignored him.

Jake had been expecting an instant improvement to his life. He was puzzled that things didn't seem to have changed much. After checking his hair and straightening his new shirt in the lavatory, he headed to the cafeteria. His plan was to bravely approach the table of the most popular kids and take a seat with them. Then, he hoped, they would accept him into their circle.

Uncomfortable and nervous, Jake bought his lunch and then headed to his destination. He wanted to run away, yet he continued on his path. When the students at the table saw him approaching, they again muttered to one another. One or two snickered, and Jake began to sweat. He went to an empty part of the table and sat down, trying to smile at the table's occupants. They looked at him but did not smile back.

Now Jake was too distressed to eat, and he just stared at his tray. He watched the steam from his spaghetti fade, and he knew it was now cold and wouldn't taste good anymore. Lunch period seemed to last forever for Jake, and when it was finally over, he was relieved to get out of the cafeteria.

While the students were walking back to class, Jake spotted Darren, the star of the football team and one of the big shots in the school social scene. Darren had a reserved seat at the table where Jake had sat that day, and had been one of the people who had snickered at him.

"What do you and your friends have against me?" asked Jake. "I'm willing to dress like you, talk like you, and act like you, and you don't even give me the smallest bit of respect in return."

Darren looked at him with surprise. "That's the point," he said. "You're not you anymore. We all liked you just fine until you started pretending you were someone else."

Jake realized then that his life was never perfect, but it was pretty good until he started dressing up and putting on acts. The next day he looked and acted like he used to, but now he understood that he was better off just being himself.

 # Questions

1   What is Jake's plan for "reinventing" himself?

_____

_____

_____

_____

2   What does Jake learn at the end of the story? Does this lesson change his behavior?

_____

_____

_____

_____

3   How would you describe Darren? Do you think he'll be a friend to Jake?

_____

_____

_____

_____

Passage 1: "New Problems for New Jake"

 Answers

1. **Sample answer:** Jake hopes to change and improve his life by becoming popular at school. He thinks he can accomplish this by purchasing fancy clothing and getting a trendy haircut.

2. **Sample answer:** By the end of the story, Jake learns that people respected him for being himself but did not respect him when he tried to act like others. He stops dressing like the popular kids and returns to acting like his old self.

3. **Sample answer:** Darren is one of the most popular students at the school, but he is not a likable character at first. He snickers at and shuns Jake. However, after Jake confronts him, Darren speaks honestly to Jake. The two will probably be on friendly terms after their talk.

Passage 2

Now read this passage and answer the questions that follow.

The Tree They Couldn't See

Wilfred Kramer was known all around town as a great illusionist. He was able to perform astounding card tricks and other clever tricks, and he always knew how to play a crowd. He would advertise himself aggressively, calling out to passersby and challenging them to try to outwit him and expose his secrets—and they never could.

Kramer sought to strengthen the public's perception of him as a world-class illusionist by doing more and more ambitious tricks. One evening he bragged that he could make the tallest tree in town disappear in the blink of an eye. Of course, the people who overheard his claim scoffed at the outrageous concept. The towering oak tree in front of the courthouse was over a hundred years old and it seemed to reach into the clouds. Obviously, making an object so huge disappear was inconceivable.

However, the people were secretly fascinated by Kramer's claim. They knew he would not risk damaging his reputation unless he actually knew of some spell that might make the tree disappear. The people hoped to catch a glimpse of any activities he was doing in preparation for his great trick. They weren't disappointed. Kramer had gathered large stacks of lumber, and he spent several days hammering them together in his yard.

"What's he making?" the people asked one another. Some speculated he was building a huge curtain to cover the tree—but there wasn't enough lumber for that.

Finally, Kramer answered their questions. "I've simply built a stage where people can sit to watch my greatest illusion ever," he proclaimed, showing off a sturdy seating platform. The people were satisfied with his explanation, but they were back to not knowing what sort of trick he had in mind.

The day after completing his stage, Kramer brought a large winch mechanism to his house. Some people saw him transporting the heavy machine, and they began to wonder what he'd do with it. Winches, they knew, were used to pull heavy weights—but no winch in the world was big enough to move the oak tree. But after a day, the winch had disappeared; all that remained in Kramer's yard was the stage.

A few days later, the illusionist rented a truck and transported the wooden stage to the courthouse lawn. Then he attached a wall to the front of the stage; in the center of the wall was an opening through which anyone on the stage could clearly see the oak tree. Dozens of people gathered on the lawn to marvel at the handcrafted stage and speculate on Kramer's next move.

However, there was no next move. Kramer simply announced that his greatest trick was scheduled for that very next evening, just after sundown. When that time approached, hundreds of people lined up to reserve a seat on the stage. When they sat down, they could see plainly through the opening in the stage wall that the oak tree was still there. Kramer had not done anything to it. He was not trying to conceal it with curtains, or lug it away using winches.

When the stage was filled, Kramer appeared in front of the crowd and waved to his audience. Then he tossed a small black cloth over the opening in the wall and began to recite what sounded like magical verses. The audience sat for several minutes in anxious silence, waiting to see the result of the illusionist's greatest trick ever. Then Kramer grabbed the black cloth and pulled it down. Nobody could see the tree through the opening.

"He made the tree disappear!" the audience shouted.

Kramer never divulged the secret of his disappearing trick—well, at least not to any person. He did tell his cat, though. He explained to his cat that he'd attached the winch to the bottom of the stage. After Kramer covered up the opening in the wall, he activated the winch. Ever so slowly, the winch had pulled the stage a few inches to the left. When Kramer pulled down the cloth, the tree was still there, just not in the audience's view. It appeared to them that, at least temporarily, Wilfred Kramer had made the tallest tree in town invisible!

Questions

1   What attitude did the people of the town take toward Kramer as he prepared for his great illusion?

   A   Curiosity
   B   Suspicion
   C   Confusion
   D   Meanness

Tip

Reread the part of the story that details Kramer's preparation for the tree illusion. How did the people treat him?

2   What part of the passage provides the resolution of the plot?

   A   The beginning of his great illusion
   B   Kramer building a wooden stage for his audience
   C   Kramer explaining the illusion to his cat
   D   The introduction of Wilfred Kramer

  Tip

   The resolution of a plot ties together all the events and questions raised in the plot.
   Which of these answer choices does that?

3   In the story, Kramer proclaims, "I've simply built a stage where people can sit to watch my
     greatest illusion ever." What does this reveal about him?

     _____

     _____

     _____

     _____

 **Tip**

   Dialogue in a story can reveal many things about the characters. Read over Kramer's statement and think about the ideas he's trying to convey. What does it tell you
   about him?

   Now check your answers on the next page.

Passage 2: "The Tree They Couldn't See"

 Answers

1. A   The people of the town are eager to find out what Kramer's trick will be, so they ask one another questions and try to spy on his progress. Their attitude is curiosity.

2. C   The event that ties up the plot, answering the question of how Kramer made the tree "disappear," occurs when he explains the illusion to his cat.

3.   **Sample answer:** When Kramer uses the phrase "my greatest illusion ever," he is showing that he likes to advertise himself. Even when he's talking about something else, like a stage, he tries to hint that he's a great illusionist.

Passage 3

Now read this passage and answer the questions that follow.

An April Day
by Henry Wadsworth Longfellow

When the warm sun, that brings
Seed-time and harvest, has returned again,
'T is sweet to visit the still wood, where springs
    The first flower of the plain.

I love the season well,
When forest glades are teeming with bright forms,
Nor dark and many-folded clouds foretell
    The coming-on of storms.

From the earth's loosened mould
The sapling draws its sustenance, and thrives;
Though stricken to the heart with winter's cold,
    The drooping tree revives.

The softly-warbled song
Comes from the pleasant woods, and colored wings
Glance quick in the bright sun, that moves along
    The forest openings.

When the bright sunset fills
The silver woods with light, the green slope throws
Its shadows in the hollows of the hills,
    And wide the upland glows.

And when the eve is born,
In the blue lake the sky, o'er-reaching far,
Is hollowed out and the moon dips her horn,
    And twinkles many a star.

Inverted in the tide
Stand the gray rocks, and trembling shadows throw,
And the fair trees look over, side by side,
    And see themselves below.

Sweet April! many a thought
Is wedded unto thee, as hearts are wed;
Nor shall they fail, till, to its autumn brought,
    Life's golden fruit is shed.

 Questions

1   The poem states, "The softly-warbled song / Comes from the pleasant woods, and colored wings / Glance quick in the bright sun." What image does the narrator create in these lines?

   A   Shadows dancing in the forest
   B   Birds flying through the woods
   C   Branches swaying in the breeze
   D   Rays of sun piercing a dense forest

 Tip

   Sometimes writers try to paint pictures with their words. Think carefully about the words the narrator uses in these lines from the poem. What picture is the author trying to paint?

2   The poem states, "And the fair trees look over, side by side, / And see themselves below." What literary device does the narrator use in these lines?

   A   Simile
   B   Metaphor
   C   Personification
   D   Hyperbole

 Tip

   Authors use literary devices to make their writing more colorful and exciting. How does the author make these lines more exciting?

3   Which words best describe the mood of this poem?

   A   Exciting and adventurous
   B   Dark and foreboding
   C   Mysterious and quiet
   D   Happy and serene

Tip

Try to picture the scene the author is describing. How would you describe this scene?

4   What can you conclude about the narrator from the poem?

A   His favorite season is spring.
B   He enjoys the fall as much as the spring.
C   He was born in the month of April.
D   He likes watching storm clouds roll in.

Tip

Read all of the answer options carefully before you make your choice. If you need to, reread the poem before you choose.

Now check your answers on the next page.

Passage 3: "An April Day"

 **Answers**

1. B   The words "softly-warbled song" and "colored wings" help to paint the image of a bird flitting in and out of the woods.

2. C   In these lines, the author personifies the trees by having them gaze at their reflection.

3. D   In the poem, the author describes a spring day when flowers are beginning to bloom, birds are singing, and everything is calm and peaceful.

4. B   Answer choice A might seem correct because the narrator says, "I love the season well." However, the narrator never specifically claims that spring is his favorite season. At the end of the poem, the narrator says that his thoughts of April will not fail *until* autumn arrives ready to shed life's golden fruit. From this, readers can conclude that the narrator enjoys both spring and fall.

Passage 4

Now read this passage and answer the questions that follow.

The Adventures of Gilgamesh

The people of Babylonia felt that their king, Gilgamesh, was a mixed blessing. On one hand, he was the mightiest and most influential king in the world. He was a hero of many battles, a son of the gods, and a man of endless intelligence and insight. He had envisioned and built the city of Uruk, a marvel of architecture with towering gates and brilliantly designed buildings. In the center of Uruk was a lapis lazuli, a gemstone with the proportions of a boulder. Carved into this stone were the chronicles of Gilgamesh's many adventures. Reading them over, nobody could deny that he had earned his fame.

However, Gilgamesh was also arrogant and brash, and frequently neglected the concerns of his people in order to concentrate on himself. On occasion he was downright oppressive, and when he began to interfere in citizens' marriages, the people decided something had to be done. They flocked to the temple and prayed to their chief god, Anu, pleading with him to confront Gilgamesh and end his exploitation. Their prayers were answered with silence, though, and the people left the temple disappointedly.

The next day, a hunter named Shuja headed into the forests outside the city in search of game. As soon as he stepped into the thick, shadowy woods, he heard an animal roar that he did not recognize. It resembled a horrifying combination of the growls, hoots, whistles, and barks of a dozen different species. He heard it again, and it was closer this time. Before he could evacuate, he found himself face-to-face with a hulking wild man surrounded by a team of vicious animals.

An hour later, an exhausted Shuja returned to the city. He looked so ragged and terrified that a crowd gathered around him, inquiring what troubles had befallen him. "I encountered a wild man in the forest, training animals for warfare," Shuja explained. "His name was Enkidu, and he said Anu had dispatched him to dethrone King Gilgamesh."

A worried murmur passed through the crowd. What would happen if such a menacing creature attacked Uruk, they wondered. The prospect was even less pleasant than the prospect of Gilgamesh's continued oppression. They realized they needed to stop Enkidu, but how could they negotiate with an animal-like man? Some thought they should fight; some thought they should flee. Some thought they should surrender to the creature and some believed they could reason with it. Nobody could agree on a course of action.

"Stop this quarrelling; I'll solve this predicament," announced Shamhat, one of the most beautiful women in Uruk. The next morning she left the city's protective walls and proceeded into the forest in search of Enkidu. She found him at a watering hole where he and his supporters had camped. Shamhat approached him, and he could sense that she was not motivated by apprehension or hostility. This caught Enkidu off guard.

Shamhat addressed Enkidu with kindness and compassion, and he responded in a similarly civil manner. They spent the day together and, the next morning, she led him into Uruk as a friend, not an enemy. The people gathered around them and celebrated the cessation of his threat. Enkidu, though disoriented by the new environment, came to love the beauty, companionship, and sophistication he encountered inside the city walls. Taking up residence with some shepherds, Enkidu learned how to behave like a civilized human being.

Meanwhile, Gilgamesh had been having visions of powerful, mysterious newcomers trespassing upon his land. It was therefore no surprise to him to learn of Enkidu's presence in Uruk. Gilgamesh consulted his mother, who advised him to embrace this newcomer as a friend, because together they were destined for great accomplishments.

"*What does she know?*" Gilgamesh thought bitterly. "*I would not degrade myself by accepting some wild man as a companion.*"

And so Gilgamesh continued his oppression of the people. During a marriage celebration, Gilgamesh interfered again. He was jealous of the groom and intended to kidnap the bride. He believed he was justified in doing so because he was the ruler of Uruk, and he was comfortable with the knowledge that nobody would challenge him. But he'd forgotten about the newcomer, Enkidu, who suddenly appeared in the king's doorway and refused to allow him to break up the wedding.

"How dare you exploit your people for your own gain?" demanded Enkidu.

"How dare you question my decisions?" roared Gilgamesh, lunging forward to attack his challenger.

The two combatants struggled for hours, their powers equally balanced. Finally, Gilgamesh was able to secure an advantage in the battle, and raised a sword high over Enkidu. Instead of bringing the sword slashing down, though, he paused and then slowly lowered the weapon.

"You are a worthy opponent," he admitted, "and I was wrong to belittle you. I see the wisdom in your challenge, and I will not spoil the wedding." Gilgamesh helped Enkidu to his feet, and then they shook hands. "I think my mother was right. If you and I work together, we can accomplish great things for the people of Uruk."

Gilgamesh and Enkidu became fast friends, and they enjoyed one another's company for many weeks. Soon, however, the pair began to feel restless in the tranquil city of Uruk. They yearned for adventures in the mysterious lands outside the city walls. "Every day we reside within these walls, we grow increasingly accustomed to peace and quiet," complained Gilgamesh. "We're losing our power and energy! Another month of this and there will be nothing to separate us from regular farmers and townspeople."

Enkidu agreed enthusiastically. He'd learned the lifestyles of civilized humans, but in his soul he felt a longing to be wild and free again. "Yes!" he roared, sounding for a moment almost like a bear. "Let's strike off into the forests and find new, undiscovered horizons!"

Gilgamesh began to envision this grand new adventure. He had a faraway look on his face as though, in his imagination, he was already tromping toward a new glorious goal. For a while, he even seemed unaware that Enkidu was watching him curiously. When Enkidu finally asked, "What are you thinking about?" Gilgamesh woke abruptly from his daydream.

"Enkidu, my friend, I have conceived of the greatest adventure ever undertaken. I propose that you and I leave tomorrow for the great Cedar Forest."

Immediately, Enkidu's enthusiasm waned. His face looked timid for the first time ever when he whimpered, "But, Gilgamesh—that's the land of the demon Humbaba the Terrible. He surely would destroy any trespassers there."

Gilgamesh laughed brazenly. "Not if we destroy him first! I propose that we do battle with Humbaba, send him back to the underworld, and claim his forest for the people of Uruk!"

Enkidu was not to be convinced. "I must protest, Gilgamesh. Do not mistake me for a coward when I say this, but during my years in the forests I've heard many horrifying tales of Humbaba. I am convinced that as an enemy he is beyond parallel. I have great faith in you, and in myself, but I doubt that even together we could defeat the likes of Humbaba."

"Nonsense," laughed Gilgamesh. "Do not hamper my spirit with your doubt. Together we will find and defeat this menace, and put the legends of his invincibility to rest forever!"

 Questions

1   Why were the people of Babylon upset with King Gilgamesh?

    A   He listened to his mother's advice.
    B   He made friends with a wild man.
    C   He forbade them to pray to Anu.
    D   He interfered in wedding ceremonies.

 Tip

If you don't recall this detail, look back to the beginning of the story.

2   Why didn't Gilgamesh want to make friends with Enkidu?

   A   He was afraid of Enkidu.
   B   He thought he was better than Enkidu.
   C   He knew Enkidu wanted to be king.
   D   His mother warned against it.

Tip

Think about when Gilgamesh first learned about Enkidu. What was his attitude toward the wild man?

3   How did Enkidu change after meeting Shamhat?

   A   From peace-loving to warlike
   B   From brave to cowardly
   C   From untamed to mannerly
   D   From noble to selfish

Tip

Think about how Enkidu acted before meeting the beautiful Shamhat, and then how he transformed afterwards.

4   What kind of story is this?

   A   A myth
   B   A drama
   C   An autobiography
   D   A fairy tale

Tip

Think about the information in this story. What kind of information is it?

Now check your answers on the next page.

Passage 4: "The Adventures of Gilgamesh"

 Answers

1. D   Early in the story, the people of Uruk were very upset with King Gilgamesh because he often interfered in the people's wedding ceremonies.

2. B   Although Gilgamesh's mother advised that he make friends with Enkidu, Gilgamesh at first refused to do so. He felt that he was too good to be friends with a wild man like Enkidu.

3. C   Before meeting Shamhat, Enkidu ran untamed in the forests with the animals. By showing him kindness, Shamhat helped him transform into a mannerly citizen.

4. A   "The Adventures of Gilgamesh" is a fictional story that deals with legendary characters and dangerous situations. It most closely matches the genre of myth.

POSTTEST

Session 1

Now read this passage and answer the questions that follow. You will have forty-five minutes to complete this section of the test.

The First Emancipation

1   In January, 1863, during the Civil War, President Abraham Lincoln delivered the Emancipation Proclamation. This speech officially declared the end of slavery in America. The southern states, which considered themselves a separate nation, refused to heed Lincoln's words. However, when the war ended and the United States of America was restored, Lincoln's message of freedom applied to every state. Finally the ancient institution of slavery was demolished in America.

For his heroic achievement, Lincoln has been dubbed "The Great Emancipator." However, many people don't realize that there were emancipations in America long before 1865.

2   As far back as the 1600s, when Europeans began to colonize America, slavery was considered normal. Many countries participated in the international slave trade, and thousands of slaves were brought to the New World. At first, many slaves were treated more as indentured servants. This meant that they were forced to do labor, but were given freedom after a certain period of time. Later, slavery was officially legalized by the colonies. Then, these servants were considered true slaves, property of their masters.

3   In the 1700s, slavery was common in the North. New England, the northeastern region of the country, was actually the center of the American slave trade. Thousands of slaves were employed there in farms, docks, and shipbuilding yards. However, as the end of that century drew near, slavery in the North was shaken by the American Revolution.

4   When America's Founding Fathers began struggling to free the nation from the tyranny of the British, they realized a great irony. American Nathaniel Niles summarized the problem when he said: "Let us either cease to enslave our fellow men, or else let us cease to complain of those that would enslave us." How could a nation proclaiming all men to be equal continue to allow slavery? During the course of the Revolutionary War, slavery in the North slowly but surely collapsed.

There are many reasons why slavery was abandoned in the North around the time of the war. One reason was that Britain was making money from the international slave trade. By refusing to purchase slaves, Americans were keeping money from the British. There was also growing pressure from religious groups, most notably the Quakers, who condemned slavery and insisted that it be ceased.

5   The final, killing blow to slavery in the North came during the battles of the Revolution. During the raging conflicts in the northern colonies, both the American and the British armies competed for the support of slaves. Many American colonies declared that any slave who would fight the British would be made free; the British in turn offered freedom to slaves who fought the Americans. Thousands of slaves participated in the Revolutionary War, on both sides, and

GO ON ▶

were freed. Thousands more fled from their owners during the chaotic conflict.

6   Between 1777 and 1804, all of the colonies in the North finally abandoned the terrible institution of slavery. It would take nearly another hundred years, and another bloody war, to end slavery across all of America.

7 **TIMELINE:**
1776 – The Quakers in England and Pennsylvania require that members of their church free their slaves.
1777 – Slavery is banned in Vermont.
1780 – Massachusetts declares all men free and equal, including former slaves.
1780 – Pennsylvania passes a law to free slaves gradually.
1784 – Connecticut and Rhode Island choose to free slaves gradually.
1799 – New York follows Pennsylvania, Connecticut, and Rhode Island.
1807 – Federal law makes it illegal for Americans to participate in the slave trade.

1 According to the passage, why did slavery fade out in the North during the American Revolution?

A Slavery became illegal in England.
B Abraham Lincoln delivered the Emancipation Proclamation.
C America did not want to give money to the British.
D Colonists started having indentured servants instead.

2 Why did President Abraham Lincoln deliver the Emancipation Proclamation?

A To announce the end of slavery in America
B To ask people to think about ending slavery
C To announce the end of the Civil War
D To ask people not to participate in the Civil War

3 According to the passage, America realized a great <u>irony</u>. What does <u>irony</u> mean?

A Something that is painful
B Something that is beneficial
C Something that is costly
D Something that is contradictory

4 The passage "The First Emancipation" is an example of which type of literature?

A Drama
B Autobiography
C Nonfiction
D Legend

5 Why did the author most likely write this passage?

A To record the most recent findings about the Emancipation Proclamation
B To suggest that most Americans do not know when slavery ended
C To entertain readers with a story set during the American Revolution
D To explain that slavery started fading out before the Civil War

GO ON ▶

Now read this passage and answer the questions that follow.

Excerpt from *The Prince and the Pauper*
by Mark Twain

1   London was fifteen hundred years old, and was a great town—for that day. It had a hundred thousand inhabitants—some think double as many. The streets were very narrow, and crooked, and dirty, especially in the part where Tom Canty lived, which was not far from London Bridge. The houses were of wood, with the second story projecting over the first, and the third sticking its elbows out beyond the second. The higher the houses grew, the broader they grew. They were skeletons of strong criss-cross beams, with solid material between, coated with plaster. The beams were painted red or blue or black, according to the owner's taste, and this gave the houses a very picturesque look. The windows were small, glazed with little diamond-shaped panes, and they opened outward, on hinges, like doors.

2   The house which Tom's father lived in was up a foul little pocket called Offal Court, out of Pudding Lane. It was small, decayed, and rickety, but it was packed full of wretchedly poor families. Canty's tribe occupied a room on the third floor. The mother and father had a sort of bedstead in the corner; but Tom, his grandmother, and his two sisters, Bet and Nan, were not restricted—they had all the floor to themselves, and might sleep where they chose. There were the remains of a blanket or two, and some bundles of ancient and dirty straw, but these could not rightly be called beds, for they were not organised; they were kicked into a general pile, mornings, and selections made from the mass at night, for service. . . .

3   No, Tom's life went along well enough, especially in summer. He only begged just enough to save himself, for the laws against mendicancy[1] were stringent, and the penalties heavy; so he put in a good deal of his time listening to good Father Andrew's charming old tales and legends about giants and fairies, dwarfs and genii, and enchanted castles, and gorgeous kings and princes. His head grew to be full of these wonderful things, and many a night as he lay in the dark on his scant and offensive straw, tired, hungry, and smarting from a thrashing, he unleashed his imagination and soon forgot his aches and pains in delicious picturings to himself of the charmed life of a petted prince in a regal palace . . .

4   He often read the priest's old books and got him to explain and enlarge upon them. His dreamings and readings worked certain changes in him, by-and-by. His dream-people were so fine that he grew to lament his shabby clothing and his dirt, and to wish to be clean and better clad. He went on playing in the mud just the same, and enjoying it, too; but, instead of splashing around in the Thames solely for the fun of it, he began to find an added value in it because of the washings and cleansings it afforded . . .

5   By-and-by Tom's reading and dreaming about princely life wrought such a strong effect upon him that he began to ACT the prince, unconsciously. His speech and

[1]**mendicancy:** begging

GO ON ▶

manners became curiously ceremonious and courtly, to the vast admiration and amusement of his intimates. But Tom's influence among these young people began to grow now, day by day; and in time he came to be looked up to, by them, with a sort of wondering awe, as a superior being. He seemed to know so much! and he could do and say such marvellous things! and withal, he was so deep and wise! Tom's remarks, and Tom's performances, were reported by the boys to their elders; and these, also, presently began to discuss Tom Canty, and to regard him as a most gifted and extraordinary creature. Full-grown people brought their perplexities to Tom for solution, and were often astonished at the wit and wisdom of his decisions. In fact he was become a hero to all who knew him except his own family—these, only, saw nothing in him.

GO ON ▶

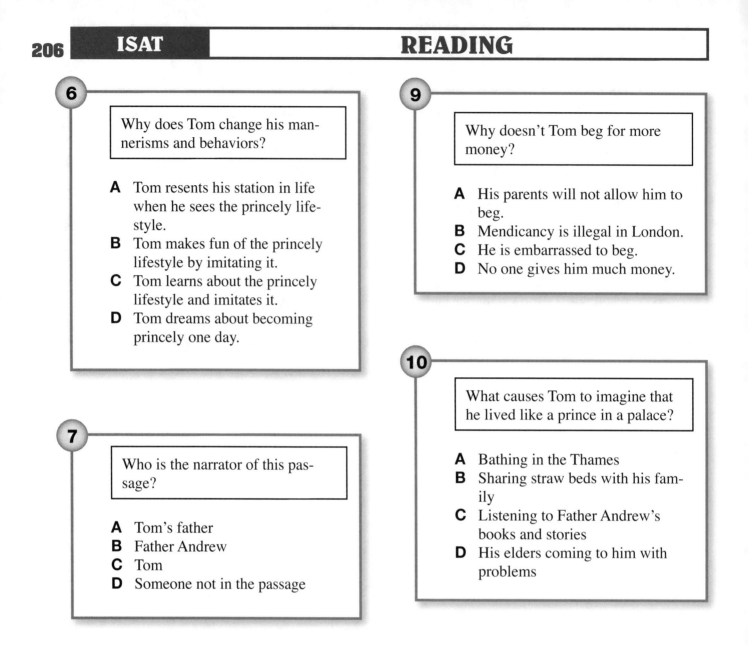

6 Why does Tom change his mannerisms and behaviors?

A Tom resents his station in life when he sees the princely lifestyle.
B Tom makes fun of the princely lifestyle by imitating it.
C Tom learns about the princely lifestyle and imitates it.
D Tom dreams about becoming princely one day.

7 Who is the narrator of this passage?

A Tom's father
B Father Andrew
C Tom
D Someone not in the passage

8 Why did Tom's friends and acquaintances begin to admire him?

A He begins to act and speak like a prince
B He begins to buy them things.
C He always knows what to do.
D He is princely despite his family.

9 Why doesn't Tom beg for more money?

A His parents will not allow him to beg.
B Mendicancy is illegal in London.
C He is embarrassed to beg.
D No one gives him much money.

10 What causes Tom to imagine that he lived like a prince in a palace?

A Bathing in the Thames
B Sharing straw beds with his family
C Listening to Father Andrew's books and stories
D His elders coming to him with problems

GO ON ▶

Now read this passage and answer the questions that follow.

Say Goodbye to the Cleavers

The Way We Were?

1   Households today are very different from those of the past. In the 1950s, most American families tried to model themselves after the seemingly perfect Cleavers on the television show "Leave It to Beaver." The vast majority of homes had a stay-at-home mother, who cleaned, cooked, and cared for the children, and a father who was in charge of discipline and the family finances. Fathers were said to have a "newspaper for a face" since they preferred the business section to interaction with their offspring, unless their authority was needed. Most families had many children, and mothers strove to keep their homes as spotless and "Cleaver-like" as humanly possible. Many families sat down together for a home-cooked meal each night and often had a weekly menu plan that might serve meatloaf on a particular night and fried chicken on another.

2   The problem with the "Cleaver ideal" is that it leaves little room for diversity, meaning not every family fits happily into this mold. Though some households in the 1950's may have resembled, or tried to resemble, the Cleavers' pleasant existence, the truth is many families did not have this type of lifestyle, and families today are looking less and less like the Cleavers.

Women in the Workforce

3   Though June Cleaver may have enjoyed baking cookies and doing laundry all day, many women today are not content to spend their days taking care of the household. In the 1950's, women were expected to get married, have children, and take care of the house. However, when more and more women began attending college in the 1960's and '70's, jobs that were once considered "men's work," like positions in the fields of business and medicine, started opening up to women. This represented a shift in society's idea of what women could and were expected to do. Though it might have been strange for a mother to have a job in the '50's, today it is very common. Today, more than sixty percent of families in the United States have a mother who is employed outside of the home. The real difference between the women of the 1950's and the women of today is that now women can choose to work or to stay home, and women of the "June Cleaver" era usually didn't have any options.

Mr. Mom

4   Many modern fathers are much more involved in child-rearing than their predecessors. Their roles extend far beyond discipline and include hugs, kisses, and diaper changes. In fact, in 2003 the U.S. Census reported that about 105,000 fathers are "stay-at-home" dads who have taken over the role that was traditionally held by mothers to raise their young children while their partners go to work. Even if they don't stay home with their children, dads today often help out around the house, cook for the family, and are involved in their children's school and extracurricular activities.

Breaking the Mold

5   Of course, not all families are "nuclear" like the Cleavers, meaning that they

GO ON ▶

include a mom, a dad, and their children. Some kids live with their grandparents, an aunt or uncle, or just one of their parents. Single-parent households have always existed, but today they are becoming more and more common. Some children have parents who are divorced, and they spend a certain amount of time with one parent and then go stay with the other parent for a while. Other kids live with just their mom or their dad. While a two-parent, dual-income household may be the most common type of household today, it is certainly not the only one. According to the census, there are 2 million single fathers and about 10 million single mothers in the United States. It's easy to see that fitting the modern family into an old-fashioned stereotype is like trying to put a square peg into a round hole. Americans do not want to be the Cleavers anymore.

GO ON ▶

11

How do families today differ from those of the past?

A Families today have more children.
B Families today share a meal each night.
C Most mothers today are in charge of disciplining.
D Most mothers today work outside of the home.

12

Why does the author believe that the "Cleaver ideal" of the past doesn't work for today's families?

A Not all families fit into this mold.
B The Cleavers were a TV family.
C Most families don't include a mother and a father.
D Today, more women go to college.

13

The passage says that "Fitting the modern family into an old-fashioned stereotype is like <u>trying to put a square peg into a round hole</u>." What does this mean?

A Families today are more square than round.
B Families today are more well-rounded than those in the past.
C Families today care more about money than family.
D Families today don't conform to the "Cleaver ideal."

14

What is probably the main reason for the shift in society's idea of what women could and were expected to do?

A More women stood up to their husbands.
B More women began attending college.
C People watched less television.
D "Leave It to Beaver" was cancelled.

15

The passage "Say Goodbye to the Cleavers" is an example of which type of literature?

A Essay
B Autobiography
C Science fiction
D Fable

GO ON ▶

Now read this passage and answer the questions that follow.

The Lamplighter
by Robert Louis Stevenson

My tea is nearly ready and the sun has left the sky.
It's time to take the window to see Leerie going by;
For every night at teatime and before you take your seat,
With lantern and with ladder he comes posting up the street.

5
Now Tom would be a driver and Maria go to sea,
And my papa's a banker and as rich as he can be;
But I, when I am stronger and can choose what I'm to do,
O Leerie, I'll go round at night and light the lamps with you!

For we are very lucky, with a lamp before the door,
10
And Leerie stops to light it as he lights so many more;
And oh! before you hurry by with ladder and with light;
O Leerie, see a little child and nod to him to-night!

16

Which is the best summary of this passage?

A   A child looks out the window each night.
B   A child wants to see a lamplighter.
C   A child wonders what to be when he grows up.
D   A man named Leerie lights lamps.

17

What happens every night at teatime?

A   The narrator goes to bed.
B   The lamplighter gathers his lantern and ladder.
C   The lamplighter walks down the street.
D   Tom and Maria play games.

18

The passage "The Lamplighter" is an example of which type of literature?

A   Myth
B   Drama
C   Poem
D   Legend

19

How does the narrator probably feel when the lamplighter walks by his window?

A   Annoyed
B   Excited
C   Indifferent
D   Angry

20

The passage says that it's time to take the window. What does this mean?

A   This is the time of night they look out the window.
B   This is the time of night they shut the curtains.
C   This is the time of year they change the windows.
D   This is the time of night they open the windows.

GO ON ▶

Now read this passage and answer the questions that follow.

The Royal Cemetery at Ur

1   In the 1920s, a team of archaeologists led by Sir Leonard Woolley made an amazing discovery. They excavated an ancient cemetery in what was once Mesopotamia, an area between the Tigris and Euphrates Rivers, most of which is now modern-day Iraq, Kuwait, and Saudi Arabia. The cemetery was located in the ancient Sumerian city-state Ur, which existed over 3,000 years ago. The Sumerians used the cemetery for over 500 years and it contained about 1,800 bodies and many ancient artifacts. Archaeologists have learned a great deal about the Sumerians and life in ancient times from studying the contents of burial tombs at Ur.

2   Most people buried in the Royal Cemetery at Ur were common citizens whose funeral rites consisted of merely wrapping their bodies in a reed mat before burial. About sixteen bodies were buried in "royal tombs," large elaborate underground structures with several rooms called chambers. Royal families— kings, queens, and their families—were buried in these tombs. The Sumerians closely intertwined politics and religion and they considered these individuals to be of great importance. Each Sumerian city-state was ruled by a king, who was also a priest. The Sumerians believed that everything around them was controlled by a god. They believed that the sun, moon, and stars were gods. They also believed that their kings were gods and that they were put on the earth to serve them. They built magnificent burial chambers for their kings and queens because they thought this would please them.

3   The Sumerians believed that kings and queens could take things with them on their journey to the afterlife. They filled royal tombs with everything they thought people would need on this journey, including clothes, jewelry, riches, weapons—and even people. It was not uncommon for Sumerian citizens to sacrifice themselves because they believed this would allow them to accompany their king in the afterlife, where they could continue to serve him.

4   Perhaps the most amazing discovery in the Cemetery at Ur was Queen Puabi's tomb. The queen's tomb was especially valuable because it was discovered intact, meaning it had not been disturbed since the Sumerians closed it thousands of years ago. Queen Puabi's tomb was built on top of another burial chamber, probably the king's. Not much is known about the king, however, because his tomb was *looted*, or robbed, many years ago, probably when the queen was buried.

5   Queen Puabi's tomb was extraordinary and demonstrated the Sumerians' advanced skills in architectural design. Her body was laid to rest on a table in the middle of an arched chamber in the center of what archaeologists refer to as a death pit. The pit and her burial chamber were filled with exquisite ancient artifacts. Queen Puabi was adorned with an incredible headdress made of gold leaves, ribbons, and strands of beads made from rare stones. She wore a

GO ON ▶

cylindrical seal around her neck bearing her name. Her name was carved into the cylinder using cuneiform, the world's first written language, which was invented by the Sumerians. The queen's body was covered in a beaded cape made from precious metals and stone. The cape stretched from her shoulders to her waist. Beautiful rings were carefully placed on each of her fingers.

6   Members of the queen's "burial party" were discovered in the death pit. Members of this burial party apparently accompanied the queen into her tomb. Each member of the party dressed formally for the special occasion and enjoyed an enormous feast prior to joining Queen Puabi. The burial party included more than a dozen attendants or servants, five armed men, a wooden sled, and a pair of oxen. Four grooms were buried with the oxen, possibly to care for the oxen in the afterlife.

7   What happened to the members of the burial party to cause their demise? No one is sure, since they died thousands of years ago. However, Sir Woolley and his teams discovered a gold cup near each of their bodies. They suspect that the attendants probably drank poison so they could go to sleep forever alongside their queen, who may or may not have already been dead.

GO ON ▶

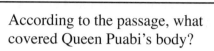
21

Why did the Sumerians build elaborate burial tombs for the kings?

A They hoped to serve their kings in the afterlife.
B They believed their kings were gods.
C They thought their kings would return one day.
D They wanted to protect their kings from thieves.

22

What was special about Queen Puabi's tomb?

A It was hidden in a chamber underground.
B It was above a king's tomb.
C It was untouched for many years.
D It contained the queen's body.

23

Why did the burial party come into the tomb with Queen Puabi?

A To punish the Sumerians when Queen Puabi died
B To protect Queen Puabi from evil spirits
C To make sure Queen Puabi didn't come back to life
D To take care of Queen Puabi in the afterlife

24

According to the passage, what covered Queen Puabi's body?

A A cylindrical seal
B A beaded cape
C Gold leaves and ribbons
D Wooden planks

25

How were common Sumerian citizens buried in the Royal Cemetery at Ur?

A They were buried with their oxen.
B They were placed in an arched chamber.
C They were wrapped in a reed mat.
D They were placed in a large tomb.

GO ON ▶

Now read this passage and answer the questions that follow.

Excerpt from *My Antonia*
by Willa Cather

1   When we reached the level and could see the gold tree-tops, I pointed toward them, and Antonia laughed and squeezed my hand as if to tell me how glad she was I had come. We raced off toward Squaw Creek and did not stop until the ground itself stopped—fell away before us so abruptly that the next step would have been out into the tree-tops. We stood panting on the edge of the ravine, looking down at the trees and bushes that grew below us. The wind was so strong that I had to hold my hat on, and the girls' skirts were blown out before them. Antonia seemed to like it; she held her little sister by the hand and chattered away in that language which seemed to me spoken so much more rapidly than mine. She looked at me, her eyes fairly blazing with things she could not say.

2   'Name? What name?' she asked, touching me on the shoulder. I told her my name, and she repeated it after me and made Yulka say it. She pointed into the gold cottonwood tree behind whose top we stood and said again, 'What name?'

3   We sat down and made a nest in the long red grass. Yulka curled up like a baby rabbit and played with a grasshopper. Antonia pointed up to the sky and questioned me with her glance. I gave her the word, but she was not satisfied and pointed to my eyes. I told her, and she repeated the word, making it sound like 'ice.' She pointed up to the sky, then to my eyes, then back to the sky, with movements so quick and impulsive that she distracted me, and I had no idea what she wanted. She got up on her knees and wrung her hands. She pointed to her own eyes and shook her head, then to mine and to the sky, nodding violently.

4   'Oh,' I exclaimed, 'blue; blue sky.'
She clapped her hands and murmured, 'Blue sky, blue eyes,' as if it amused her. While we snuggled down there out of the wind, she learned a score of words. She was alive, and very eager. We were so deep in the grass that we could see nothing but the blue sky over us and the gold tree in front of us. It was wonderfully pleasant. After Antonia had said the new words over and over, she wanted to give me a little chased silver ring she wore on her middle finger. When she coaxed and insisted, I repulsed her quite sternly. I didn't want her ring, and I felt there was something reckless and extravagant about her wishing to give it away to a boy she had never seen before. No wonder Krajiek got the better of these people, if this was how they behaved.

5   While we were disputing about the ring, I heard a mournful voice calling, 'Antonia, Antonia!' She sprang up like a hare. 'Tatinek! Tatinek!' she shouted, and we ran to meet the old man who was coming toward us. Antonia reached him first, took his hand and kissed it. When I came up, he touched my shoulder and looked searchingly down into my face

GO ON ▶

for several seconds. I became somewhat embarrassed, for I was used to being taken for granted by my elders.

6   We went with Mr. Shimerda back to the dugout, where grandmother was waiting for me. Before I got into the wagon, he took a book out of his pocket, opened it, and showed me a page with two alphabets, one English and the other Bohemian. He placed this book in my grandmother's hands, looked at her entreatingly, and said, with an earnestness which I shall never forget, 'Te-e-ach, te-e-ach my Antonia!'

GO ON ▶

26

What attitude did the narrator take toward the girl while they were talking?

A Curiosity
B Suspicion
C Annoyance
D Meanness

27

Why does the narrator refuse Antonia's ring?

A He doesn't think boys should wear rings.
B He thinks her father will be mad if he takes it.
C He doesn't think she should give her ring to a stranger.
D He thinks his mother will make him give it back.

28

Why does Mr. Shimerda show the book to the narrator's grandmother?

A He wants her to teach his daughter English.
B He wants to show her his alphabet.
C He wants her to learn his language.
D He wants her to read to him.

29

What can you conclude about Antonia?

A She doesn't like to meet people.
B She wants to learn English.
C She does not respect her parents.
D She is not good with people.

30

The passage states that Antonia pointed up to the sky, then to the narrator's eyes, then back to the sky, with quick and impulsive movements. What does impulsive mean?

A Leisurely and logical
B Neat and organized
C Fashionable and trendy
D Rapid and without thought

STOP

Session 2

Now read this passage and answer the questions that follow. You will have forty-five minutes to complete this session.

Space Colonization: Too Big a Risk

1   Just a few decades ago, the idea of establishing colonies in space was viewed as nothing more than a wild science-fiction tale. However, as technological advances and scientific discoveries teach us more about the places beyond our planet, space colonization looks increasingly possible. Within our lifetimes, we may see people making an effort to build a permanent city on another planet or even on an asteroid. Perhaps you or I will even travel to the stars for a vacation!

2   If you were able to vote today on whether or not another planet—the red planet Mars, for instance—should be colonized, would you vote "yes" or "no"? Many people are enthusiastic about this idea, and see it as an entirely positive opportunity for the people of Earth. These supporters of space colonization have many good ideas, but may be overlooking some other important information. Colonizing another planet would be one of the biggest steps ever taken in human history. An accomplishment that important carries along many dangers, expenses, and other concerns. Before you make your decision, you should be aware of the possible negative aspects of such an event.

3   First of all, the complications of establishing a livable city on another planet

are staggering. Even the world's finest scientists are still baffled by the question of how they could keep people safe and healthy on the surface of an alien world. People require very special conditions in order to live, and it would be hard to ensure those conditions on an unexplored new world.

4   Of all the planets, Mars seems like it would best support human visitors—but it's still an inhospitable place. The atmosphere is so thin it would be impossible to breathe. People would need special equipment in order to get the air they need to live. It's possible that the first colonists would have to spend their entire lives wearing space suits. Also, temperatures on the red planet can become extremely cold—much colder than Antarctica. It might be possible for people to live in such temperatures, but few would find them comfortable!

5   Although there may have once been flowing water on Mars, today it is a very dry planet. Humans rely on water to live, and colonists would have to bring a large amount of it with them. Special machines would have to be developed in order to recycle the drinking water. Even if the water problem was solved, how would the colonists get food? The Martian ground is rocky and dry; it seems unlikely that any kind of Earth crops could possibly grow there. Until that was figured out, rockets would have to be constantly sent to the colony with fresh supplies; the cost of doing this would be huge.

6   Additionally, the overall cost of a colonization mission would be downright breathtaking. Scientists have estimated the price tag of a single mission to be set at about

$30 billion. That funding is desperately needed for projects here on our planet. Social programs of all sorts could benefit greatly from even a fraction of that amount. We humans would be wise to invest more time, money, and effort into improving our own world before we start visiting others.

7   That idea leads into one of the saddest but most important questions we must keep in mind during this age of amazing new technologies: can humans be trusted with a brand new planet? Humans have proven to be very imperfect guests, to say the least. The greatest threats to our current planet are posed by us, its inhabitants. Through weapons, warfare, pollution, and greed, humanity has taken advantage of the natural splendor that Earth once possessed. Some scientists believe that humans have a duty to spread out across the solar system and spread beauty and intelligence. However, over the centuries humans have spread just as much hatred and horror as they've spread beauty and intelligence. Infecting a new planet with human problems would be an abominable thing to do.

8   Some supporters of space colonization believe that the nations of Earth would unify and work together to achieve this common goal. These supporters think that all aspects of Earth life, from education to economics, would be improved by the race to colonize space. However, a short survey of history points to opposite ideas.

9   History shows that colonization has caused greed, hatred, prejudice and war among the nations of Earth. Imagine the effects of space colonization! Nations would likely struggle to be first to reach the red planet; then they would struggle for the rights to build on the best land; then they would struggle for resources for their colonists. The results could be more mistrust, fear, and conflict. A Mars colony might end up further dividing the people of Earth and yielding more suffering than discovery.

10   Should a colonization project proceed despite these many problems, what sort of benefits would it bring to the people of Earth? Some scientists have suggested that we build mines in space to gather valuable metals like iron and gold from asteroids and other celestial bodies. This would return some of the costs of the mission. However, our planet is already well equipped with dozens of types of metal and minerals. In fact, with Earth's natural resources as well as our recycling programs, we have more than enough already. Besides, if we were to build colonies just to make money, greedy competition would no doubt arise that would endanger the whole project.

11   Some scientists have proclaimed that colonizing the red planet would ensure the survival of the human race. Their argument is that, even if Earth were to die or be destroyed, a group of humans would still exist in their Martian colony. This argument may be true, but it's not a strong argument because it doesn't apply to our world's current situation. Earth is still a healthy and vital planet and promises to remain that way for a very long time. The human race is growing every year and is definitely not endangered. We humans can live on for millions of years longer on Earth, if only we learn to behave more responsibly.

12   In conclusion, the concept of space colonization is a fascinating one, but it is fraught with problems and dangers. There may be a time when humans are ready to build their cities on the surface of Mars. However, attempting to conquer Mars now, while neglecting Earth, might bring enormous damage to Earth and its inhabitants.

GO ON ▶

31

What is the author's strongest argument against space colonization?

A He is fearful that something bad will happen.
B He thinks the cost is simply ridiculous.
C He thinks that human beings will be in danger.
D He thinks it will stir up conflict with other nations.

32

Why does the author believe that the human race will survive on Earth for many more years to come?

A The population is increasing.
B Technology is advancing quickly.
C Medical advances are being made.
D Conflict among nations has been reduced.

33

Where would human beings living on Mars get the water they needed to survive?

A They would carry large tanks containing water.
B They would have to bring water from Earth.
C They would have to drill for water on Mars.
D They would have to search for water on nearby planets.

34

The passage says that until a few years ago, people considered space colonization a <u>wild science-fiction tale</u>. What does this mean?

A People believed that space colonization would be an incredible adventure.
B People did not believe that space colonization would ever happen.
C People believed that only the most fortunate would get to live in space.
D People did not understand the details of space colonization.

35

According to the passage, Mars is an <u>inhospitable</u> place. What does <u>inhospitable</u> mean?

A Far away
B Exceptionally warm
C Not welcoming
D Not smooth

GO ON ▶

36 Which best describes the author's message in this passage?

A People would need too much special equipment to be able to live on Mars.
B We should only travel to Mars to go on a vacation.
C People should focus on improving life on Earth rather than moving to Mars.
D We should not live on Mars because there is no water on the planet.

37 Why does the author believe that space colonization will cause international conflict?

A Nations will compete with each other.
B Nations will be unwilling to share the planet.
C Nations will not trust one another.
D Nations will not focus on the problems on Earth.

38 How is the atmosphere on Mars different from the atmosphere on Earth?

A It is cloudy.
B It contains gas.
C It is thinner.
D It is toxic.

39 Which is an example of alliteration?

A "People require very special conditions in order to live."
B "The Martian ground is rocky and dry."
C "Humans have spread as much hatred and horror as they've spread beauty and intelligence."
D "The human race is growing every year."

40 According to the author, which best describes modern scientists' knowledge of space colonization?

A In-depth
B Limited
C Faulty
D Advanced

41 According to the passage, how might space colonists make up for some of the cost of space colonization?

A By telling their story
B By mining for minerals
C By giving tours
D By learning about Earth

GO ON ▶

42

What is the estimated cost of a single mission to Mars?

A $30 trillion
B $30 billion
C $30 million
D $30 thousand

43

The author of the passage states that infecting a new planet with human problems would be an <u>abominable</u> thing to do. What does <u>abominable</u> mean?

A Easy
B Comforting
C Terrible
D Safe

44

Why does the author believe Mars isn't needed for the survival of the human race?

A Earth is still healthy.
B Nobody wants to live on Mars.
C Mars cannot ever be colonized.
D Humans will destroy themselves.

45

According to the passage, what would happen if colonists began mines on Mars?

A People would stop using Earth's resources.
B Scientists would find out Mars' resources are unsafe.
C Greed and competition would arise and ruin the project.
D The colonists would be too busy mining to study the planet.

46

The passage "Space Colonization: Too Big a Risk" is an example of what type of literature?

A Science fiction
B Essay
C Tragedy
D Biography

GO ON ▶

47

Do you agree with the author's belief that a Mars colonization project would be a bad idea?
Use information from the passage to explain your answer.

Now read this passage and answer the questions that follow.

How to Set Up an Aquarium

1   Over the last century, fish have consistently been one of America's most preferred pets. Compared to most popular domestic animals, fish are low-maintenance creatures. They're well-behaved, too. It's hard to imagine a fish gnawing on furniture, shredding curtains, or shedding fur!

2   Setting up an aquarium can be an enjoyable project that calls on you to not only choose the conditions that would most benefit the fish, but also to make creative decisions that make the aquarium a piece of aquatic art. In order to construct an aquarium that's safe for fish and pleasing to the eye, follow these general guidelines. For more specific information, consult a specialist at your local pet shop.

3   **What You'll Need**
- Aquarium (glass or plastic)
- Water
- Filter
- Water Heater
- Water Pump
- Gravel
- Fish
- Fish Food

4   **NOTE:** Aquariums come in a wide variety of shapes and sizes, from the traditional goldfish bowl to massive tanks equitable in size to some rooms. In selecting an appropriately sized aquarium, consider how many fish you intend to keep in it. To allow your fish to live comfortably, you should generally provide at least one gallon of water per fish.

5   Once you've acquired the necessary materials, the first step is to cleanse the aquarium of any grime, sediments, or other refuse that may have accumulated in it. Avoid using cleaning chemicals, though, since they can contaminate the water you later add to the aquarium. Once the aquarium is clean, add gravel to the

GO ON ▶

bottom, typically one pound per gallon of water. You can even accessorize your aquarium with rocks or plants.

6   You'll want to install a filter in order to remove contaminants from the water and keep your fish healthy. Select a filter that's suitable for the size of your aquarium, and then install it according to the directions.

7   The next step is to fill the aquarium with clean, cool water; a safe guideline here is to only utilize water that you would consider drinkable. Don't fill the aquarium right to the top, though, because there are still a few subsequent items you'll need to add, including the water heater and pump. Install these appliances according to their directions. Usually, the heater should be adjusted to keep the water at a temperature of about seventy-five degrees Fahrenheit.

      Then the fish will be more comfortable

8   and healthy—unless you forget to add them! The most crucial component of an aquarium is, of course, the fish. Add them to the water and enjoy your new finned friends.

GO ON ▶

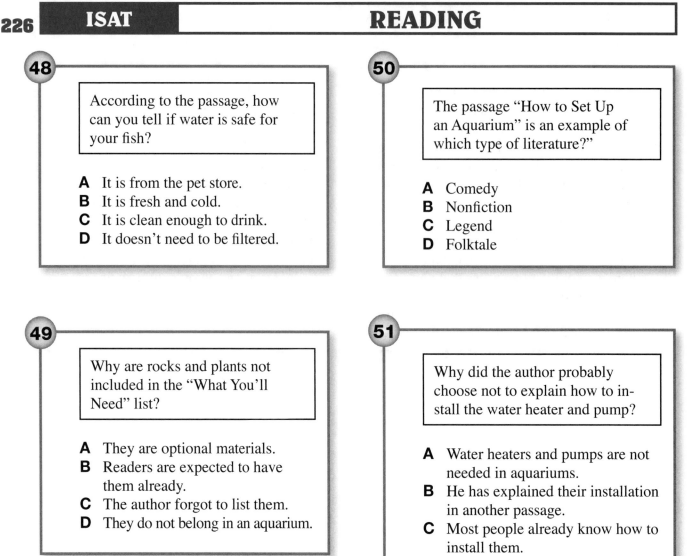

48

According to the passage, how can you tell if water is safe for your fish?

A It is from the pet store.
B It is fresh and cold.
C It is clean enough to drink.
D It doesn't need to be filtered.

50

The passage "How to Set Up an Aquarium" is an example of which type of literature?"

A Comedy
B Nonfiction
C Legend
D Folktale

49

Why are rocks and plants not included in the "What You'll Need" list?

A They are optional materials.
B Readers are expected to have them already.
C The author forgot to list them.
D They do not belong in an aquarium.

51

Why did the author probably choose not to explain how to install the water heater and pump?

A Water heaters and pumps are not needed in aquariums.
B He has explained their installation in another passage.
C Most people already know how to install them.
D Water heaters and pumps come with their own directions.

STOP

Session 3

Now read this passage and answer the questions that follow. You will have forty-five minutes to complete this session.

The Secret Garden

from Chapter 15 — "Nest Building"
by Frances Hodgson Burnett

1   After another week of rain the high arch of blue sky appeared again and the sun which poured down was quite hot. Though there had been no chance to see either the secret garden or Dickon, Mistress Mary had enjoyed herself very much. The week had not seemed long. She had spent hours of every day with Colin in his room, talking about Rajahs or gardens or Dickon and the cottage on the moor. They had looked at the splendid books and pictures and sometimes Mary had read things to Colin, and sometimes he had read a little to her. When he was amused and interested she thought he scarcely looked like an invalid at all, except that his face was so colorless and he was always on the sofa. . . .

2   In her talks with Colin, Mary had tried to be very cautious about the secret garden. There were certain things she wanted to find out from him, but she felt that she must find them out without asking him direct questions. In the first place, as she began to like to be with him, she wanted to discover whether he was the kind of boy you could tell a secret to. He was not in the least like Dickon, but he was evidently so pleased with the idea of a garden no one knew anything about that she thought perhaps he could be trusted. But she had not known him long enough to be sure. The second thing she wanted to find out was this: If he could be trusted—if he really could—wouldn't it be possible to take him to the garden

without having anyone find it out? The grand doctor had said that he must have fresh air and Colin had said that he would not mind fresh air in a secret garden. Perhaps if he had a great deal of fresh air and knew Dickon and the robin and saw things growing he might not think so much about dying. Mary had seen herself in the glass sometimes lately when she had realized that she looked quite a different creature from the child she had seen when she arrived from India. This child looked nicer. Even Martha had seen a change in her.

3   "Th' air from th' moor has done thee good already," she had said. "Tha'rt not nigh so yeller and tha'rt not nigh so scrawny. Even tha' hair doesn't slamp down on tha' head so flat. It's got some life in it so as it sticks out a bit."

4   "It's like me," said Mary. "It's growing stronger and fatter. I'm sure there's more of it."

5   "It looks it, for sure," said Martha, ruffling it up a little round her face. "Tha'rt not half so ugly when it's that way an' there's a bit o' red in tha' cheeks."

6   If gardens and fresh air had been good for her perhaps they would be good for Colin. But then, if he hated people to look at him, perhaps he would not like to see Dickon.

7   "Why does it make you angry when you are looked at?" she inquired one day.

8   "I always hated it," he answered, "even when I was very little. Then when they took me to the seaside and I used to lie in my carriage everybody used to stare and ladies would stop and talk to my nurse and then they would begin to whisper and I knew then they were saying I shouldn't live to grow up. Then sometimes the ladies would pat my cheeks and say 'Poor child!' Once when a lady did that I screamed out loud and bit her hand. She was so frightened she ran away."

9   "She thought you had gone mad like a dog," said Mary, not at all admiringly.

10   "I don't care what she thought," said Colin, frowning.

11   "I wonder why you didn't scream and bite me when I came into your room?" said Mary. Then she began to smile slowly.

12   "I thought you were a ghost or a dream," he said. "You can't bite a ghost or a dream, and if you scream they don't care."

13   "Would you hate it if—if a boy looked at you?" Mary asked uncertainly.

14   He lay back on his cushion and paused thoughtfully.

15   "There's one boy," he said quite slowly, as if he were thinking over every word, "there's one boy I believe I shouldn't mind. It's that boy who knows where the foxes live—Dickon."

         . . .

16   On that first morning when the sky was blue again Mary wakened very early. The sun was pouring in slanting rays through the blinds and there was something so joyous in the sight of it that she jumped out of bed and ran to the window. She drew up the blinds and opened the window itself and a great waft of fresh, scented air blew in upon her. The moor was blue and the whole world looked as if something Magic had happened to it. There were tender little fluting sounds here and there and everywhere, as if scores of birds were beginning to tune up for a concert. Mary put her hand out of the window and held it in the sun.

17   "It's warm—warm!" she said. "It will make the green points push up and up and up, and it will make the bulbs and roots work and struggle with all their might under the earth."

18   She kneeled down and leaned out of the window as far as she could, breathing big breaths and sniffing the air until she laughed because she remembered what Dickon's mother had said about the end of his nose quivering like a rabbit's. "It must be very early," she said. "The little clouds are all pink and I've never seen the sky look like this. No one is up. I don't even hear the stable boys."

18   A sudden thought made her scramble to her feet.

20   "I can't wait! I am going to see the garden!"

21   She had learned to dress herself by this time and she put on her clothes in five minutes. She knew a small side door which she could unbolt herself and she flew downstairs in her stocking feet and put on her shoes in the hall. She unchained and unbolted and unlocked and when the door was open she sprang across the step with one bound, and there she was standing on the grass, which

GO ON ▶

seemed to have turned green, and with the sun pouring down on her and warm sweet wafts about her and the fluting and twittering and singing coming from every bush and tree. She clasped her hands for pure joy and looked up in the sky and it was so blue and pink and pearly and white and flooded with springtime light that she felt as if she must flute and sing aloud herself and knew that thrushes and robins and skylarks could not possibly help it. She ran around the shrubs and paths towards the secret garden.

22 "It is all different already," she said. "The grass is greener and things are sticking up everywhere and things are uncurling and green buds of leaves are showing. This afternoon I am sure Dickon will come."

23 The long warm rain had done strange things to the herbaceous beds which bordered the walk by the lower wall. There were things sprouting and pushing out from the roots of clumps of plants and there were actually here and there glimpses of royal purple and yellow unfurling among the stems of crocuses. Six months before Mistress Mary would not have seen how the world was waking up, but now she missed nothing.

GO ON ▶

52

According to Martha, what about Mary has changed?

A She is less bossy.
B She looks better.
C She isn't as pretty.
D She doesn't play outside anymore.

53

In the passage, the reader is told that Mary and Colin "looked at the <u>splendid</u> books and pictures." Which means the same as <u>splendid</u>?

A Wonderful
B Boring
C Educational
D Helpful

54

What is the theme of this passage?

A It's better to have loved and lost than never to have loved at all.
B Believe in the magical healing and renewing powers of nature.
C It is sometimes wise to read between the lines.
D People should not believe everything that they hear.

55

The narrator says, "Six months before Mistress Mary would not have seen how the world was waking up, but now she missed nothing." What does this mean?

A Mary would have been in India six months ago.
B Mary would have enjoyed the winter six months ago.
C Mary would not have been paying attention six months ago.
D Mary would not have been outside six months ago.

56

From which point of view is this passage told?

A First person
B Third person
C Omniscient
D Limited omniscient

57

What is this passage mostly about?

A Mary is trying to get Colin and Dickon to be friends.
B Mary wants to get Colin outside so the garden can help him, too.
C Mary is missing Dickon.
D Mary wants to do something outside.

GO ON ▶

58

Why didn't Colin scream or bite Mary when she came into his room?

A He already knew her.
B She was younger than the ladies at the beach.
C He was asleep when she came in.
D He thought she was a ghost or a dream.

59

Why are "strange things" happening in the garden now?

A Dickon has been planting flowers.
B Mary hasn't seen the garden since the winter.
C The rain has caused things to begin to grow.
D Animals have eaten a bunch of the plants.

60

At the beginning of the passage, why are Colin and Mary reading inside?

A It is raining.
B They are studying for school.
C It's cold outside.
D They prefer reading to the outdoors.

61

What is the relationship between Mary and Colin?

A They are friends.
B Mary is Colin's tutor.
C They are brother and sister.
D They are cousins.

62

Why did the author most likely write this passage?

A To entertain the reader
B To educate the reader about gardens
C To inform the reader how plants grow
D To persuade the reader to grow a garden

63

The narrator says that there were "glimpses of royal purple and yellow <u>unfurling</u> among the stems of crocuses." What does <u>unfurling</u> mean?

A Moving
B Opening
C Closing
D Falling

GO ON ▶

64

Why does Colin get angry when people look at him?

A People laugh at him.
B People make fun of his face.
C People stare at him.
D People are afraid of him.

65

Why does Mary want to know if Colin can be trusted?

A She wants to tell him about India.
B She wants to take him to the garden.
C She wants to introduce him to Dickon.
D She wants to tell him about her parents.

66

Based on what you have read, do you think that Mary will take Colin to the garden? Why or why not? Support your answer with examples from the passage.

GO ON ▶

Now read this passage and answer the questions that follow.

Come to Camp Wallabe!

1　Stifling in the sticky city heat? Seen the same summer sights over and over again? It's time to abandon your apartment, gather up your gear, and head to Camp Wallabe for some summertime fun!

2　Located along the pristine shores of Haida Lake, Camp Wallabe offers a diverse selection of summer activities that are sure to satisfy every camper. Choose one of two five-week programs offered between the months of June and August to campers ages five to sixteen.

3　**Location**—The lakeside grounds of Camp Wallabe are cared for by campers. Teaching children to respect their environment by cleaning up after themselves and by caring for the natural resources around them is an important part of the Camp Wallabe experience.

4　Participating in various exciting activities on the camp's extensive grounds becomes a reward for the hard work necessary to keep our camp clean.

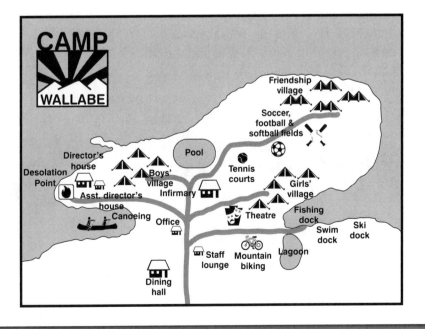

GO ON ▶

5   **Activities**—Camp Wallabe offers more activities for campers than any other facility in the area.

6   **Swimming**—Beginning to intermediate swimmers can cool off all summer long in one of the camp's two pools, or in refreshing Haida Lake itself. Our counselors are all certified lifeguards trained in swimming instruction, CPR, and First Aid. Campers can participate in swimming instruction or enjoy leisure swims during lifeguard hours. Advanced swimmers may perform in program-long structured aquatic competitions.

11   **Boating/Fishing**—Counselor-supervised boating activities include kayaking, canoeing, sailing, and fishing. At the end of each program, campers may participate in a day-long fishing adventure that ends with a fish fry on the beach. Campers may also sign up for kayak and canoe racing in the Wallabe Wars end-of-program camp-wide competition. Campers twelve and older may also take waterskiing lessons.

Athletics—Camp Wallabe has so many

12   athletic activities you may not get to try them all! The camp has multiple facilities for playing soccer, softball, football, lacrosse, volleyball, basketball, field hockey, archery, rock climbing, and more. Campers may choose from several athletic opportunities on a daily basis.

13   **Horseback Riding**—With our own stables located on camp grounds, Camp Wallabe is an ideal place for beginning and advanced riders alike. Our stables are run by equestrian experts and house several steeds, as well as a few ponies for younger riders. Campers can go on guided trail and shoreline rides or practice guiding horses around a course, complete with small obstacles. Horses draw students in a large wagon for an end-of-summer hay ride.

GO ON ▶

14   **Theater Arts**—Many campers choose to pursue a serious summer study of the dramatic arts, attending daily acting and performance workshops to improve theatrical skills. In addition to performing weekly skits and musical compositions for campers and staff alike, campers may participate in the production of a full-length play—which also offers many behind-the-scenes opportunities for involvement—to be held at the end of each program. Students who play a musical instrument are welcome to store their instruments in secure camp facilities.

15   **Arts and Crafts**—From beaded key chains to sculpture and sofa-size paintings, Camp Wallabe is prepared to accommodate the artist in each camper. Our arts and crafts rooms are spacious and stocked with supplies. Campers may spend daily craft time creating pottery, ceramics, origami, jewelry, and papier mâché designs. Quilting and other textile activities are also favorites of many campers. Those campers who are serious about art may enroll for sketching, sculpture, photography, and oil painting classes, at an extra cost. These classes require that campers dedicate a certain amount of time each day to artistic projects to make sure that projects are completed by the end of the program. Students enrolled in these classes get preference for studio time.

Schedule

16   Each week, campers may structure their own schedules, with some flex time for trying out unscheduled activities.

17   **7:30 AM:** Rise and shine, campers!
7:45 AM: Outdoor yoga (optional)
8:00 to 9:00 AM: Breakfast/cleanup in the mess hall
9:00 to 10:30 AM: Activity 1 (from weekly schedule)
10:30 to 11:45 AM: Activity 2 (from weekly schedule)
12:00 to 1:00 PM: Lunch/cleanup in the mess hall
1:00 to 3:00 PM: Flex time (choose an activity)
3:00 to 5:00 PM: Activity 3 (from weekly schedule)
5:00 to 5:30 PM: Camp-wide cleanup
5:30 to 6:00 PM: Pre-dinner cabin time
6:00 to 7:30 PM: Dinner/cleanup in the mess hall
8:00 to 10:00 PM: Mess Hall Movie Series (wear your PJs!)
10:15 PM: Lights out.

Costs

Camper costs vary each season. Costs include meals, lodging, and most activities. Additional costs include Camp Wallabe T-shirts, sweatshirts, sweatpants, and shorts (all required). Certain art classes also carry an additional cost.

Contact the camp for the most recent prices, to sign up for special classes, and to find out more about summers at Camp Wallabe!

GO ON ▶

67

Why is Camp Wallabe an ideal place for horseback riders?

A   The staff are all professional riding instructors.
B   The horse stables are located right on the camp grounds.
C   The campers are all beginning to advanced horseback riders.
D   The camp buys show-winning horses for campers to ride.

68

Why does the author include a map with the passage?

A   To show the reader the distance from the lake to the stables
B   To show the reader where campers sleep
C   To show the reader how far the camp is from the nearest city
D   To show the reader the layout of the camp

69

Why did the author most likely write this passage?

A   To tell the reader about his experience at Camp Wallabe
B   To persuade the reader to pick Camp Wallabe over another camp
C   To tell the reader how to get to Camp Wallabe
D   To tell the reader what Camp Wallabe is like

70

The passage asks the question "Stifling in the sticky city heat?" What does stifling mean?

A   Shaking
B   Roasting
C   Itching
D   Sitting

GO ON ▶

ANSWER SHEETS

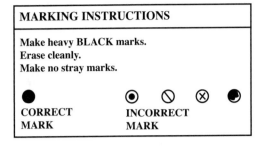
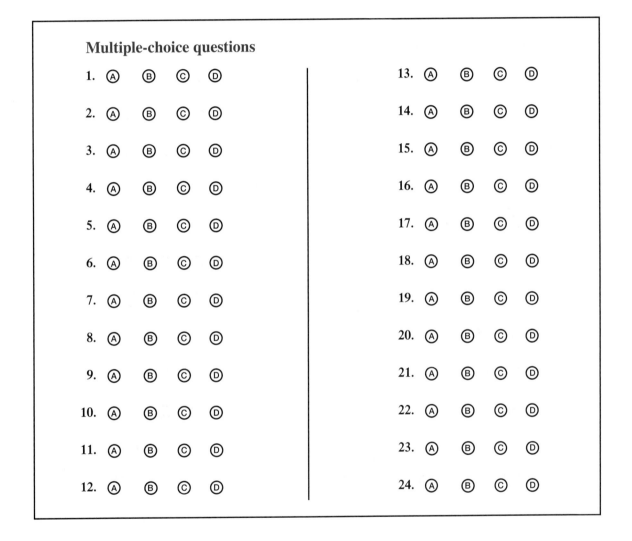

Multiple-choice questions

1. Ⓐ Ⓑ Ⓒ Ⓓ

2. Ⓐ Ⓑ Ⓒ Ⓓ

3. Ⓐ Ⓑ Ⓒ Ⓓ

4. Ⓐ Ⓑ Ⓒ Ⓓ

5. Ⓐ Ⓑ Ⓒ Ⓓ

6. Ⓐ Ⓑ Ⓒ Ⓓ

7. Ⓐ Ⓑ Ⓒ Ⓓ

8. Ⓐ Ⓑ Ⓒ Ⓓ

9. Ⓐ Ⓑ Ⓒ Ⓓ

10. Ⓐ Ⓑ Ⓒ Ⓓ

11. Ⓐ Ⓑ Ⓒ Ⓓ

12. Ⓐ Ⓑ Ⓒ Ⓓ

13. Ⓐ Ⓑ Ⓒ Ⓓ

14. Ⓐ Ⓑ Ⓒ Ⓓ

15. Ⓐ Ⓑ Ⓒ Ⓓ

16. Ⓐ Ⓑ Ⓒ Ⓓ

17. Ⓐ Ⓑ Ⓒ Ⓓ

18. Ⓐ Ⓑ Ⓒ Ⓓ

19. Ⓐ Ⓑ Ⓒ Ⓓ

20. Ⓐ Ⓑ Ⓒ Ⓓ

21. Ⓐ Ⓑ Ⓒ Ⓓ

22. Ⓐ Ⓑ Ⓒ Ⓓ

23. Ⓐ Ⓑ Ⓒ Ⓓ

24. Ⓐ Ⓑ Ⓒ Ⓓ

Student Name_____

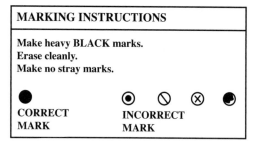

MARKING INSTRUCTIONS

Make heavy BLACK marks.
Erase cleanly.
Make no stray marks.

CORRECT
MARK

INCORRECT
MARK

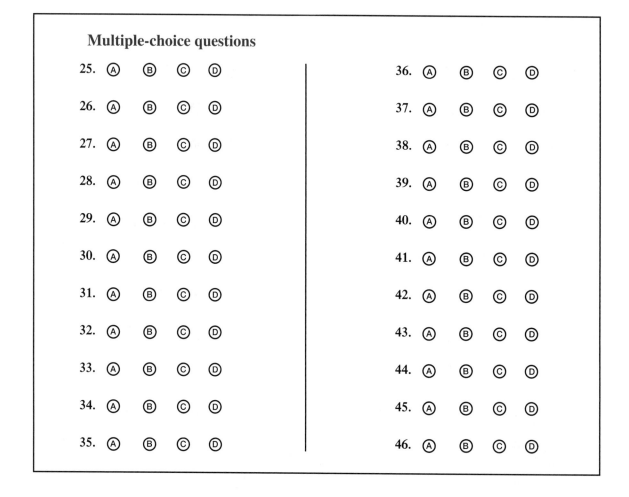

Multiple-choice questions

25.	Ⓐ	Ⓑ	Ⓒ	Ⓓ		36.	Ⓐ	Ⓑ	Ⓒ	Ⓓ
26.	Ⓐ	Ⓑ	Ⓒ	Ⓓ		37.	Ⓐ	Ⓑ	Ⓒ	Ⓓ
27.	Ⓐ	Ⓑ	Ⓒ	Ⓓ		38.	Ⓐ	Ⓑ	Ⓒ	Ⓓ
28.	Ⓐ	Ⓑ	Ⓒ	Ⓓ		39.	Ⓐ	Ⓑ	Ⓒ	Ⓓ
29.	Ⓐ	Ⓑ	Ⓒ	Ⓓ		40.	Ⓐ	Ⓑ	Ⓒ	Ⓓ
30.	Ⓐ	Ⓑ	Ⓒ	Ⓓ		41.	Ⓐ	Ⓑ	Ⓒ	Ⓓ
31.	Ⓐ	Ⓑ	Ⓒ	Ⓓ		42.	Ⓐ	Ⓑ	Ⓒ	Ⓓ
32.	Ⓐ	Ⓑ	Ⓒ	Ⓓ		43.	Ⓐ	Ⓑ	Ⓒ	Ⓓ
33.	Ⓐ	Ⓑ	Ⓒ	Ⓓ		44.	Ⓐ	Ⓑ	Ⓒ	Ⓓ
34.	Ⓐ	Ⓑ	Ⓒ	Ⓓ		45.	Ⓐ	Ⓑ	Ⓒ	Ⓓ
35.	Ⓐ	Ⓑ	Ⓒ	Ⓓ		46.	Ⓐ	Ⓑ	Ⓒ	Ⓓ

Student Name_____

Write your final response for question 47 here.

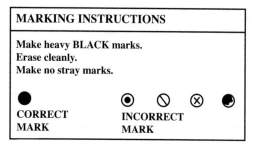

MARKING INSTRUCTIONS

Make heavy BLACK marks.
Erase cleanly.
Make no stray marks.

CORRECT MARK

INCORRECT MARK

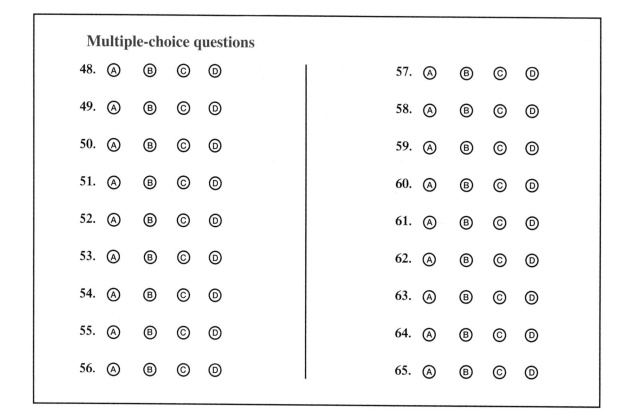

Multiple-choice questions

48. Ⓐ Ⓑ Ⓒ Ⓓ   57. Ⓐ Ⓑ Ⓒ Ⓓ

49. Ⓐ Ⓑ Ⓒ Ⓓ   58. Ⓐ Ⓑ Ⓒ Ⓓ

50. Ⓐ Ⓑ Ⓒ Ⓓ   59. Ⓐ Ⓑ Ⓒ Ⓓ

51. Ⓐ Ⓑ Ⓒ Ⓓ   60. Ⓐ Ⓑ Ⓒ Ⓓ

52. Ⓐ Ⓑ Ⓒ Ⓓ   61. Ⓐ Ⓑ Ⓒ Ⓓ

53. Ⓐ Ⓑ Ⓒ Ⓓ   62. Ⓐ Ⓑ Ⓒ Ⓓ

54. Ⓐ Ⓑ Ⓒ Ⓓ   63. Ⓐ Ⓑ Ⓒ Ⓓ

55. Ⓐ Ⓑ Ⓒ Ⓓ   64. Ⓐ Ⓑ Ⓒ Ⓓ

56. Ⓐ Ⓑ Ⓒ Ⓓ   65. Ⓐ Ⓑ Ⓒ Ⓓ

Student Name_____

Write your final response for question 66 here.

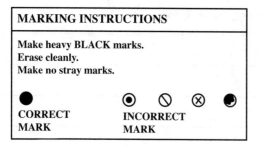

MARKING INSTRUCTIONS

Make heavy BLACK marks.
Erase cleanly.
Make no stray marks.

CORRECT
MARK

INCORRECT
MARK

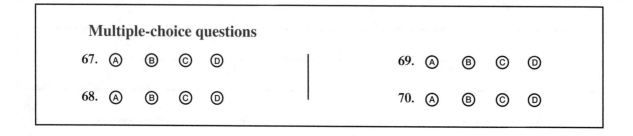

Multiple-choice questions

67. Ⓐ   Ⓑ   Ⓒ   Ⓓ   69. Ⓐ   Ⓑ   Ⓒ   Ⓓ

68. Ⓐ   Ⓑ   Ⓒ   Ⓓ   70. Ⓐ   Ⓑ   Ⓒ   Ⓓ

Student Name_____

ANSWER KEY

Answer Key
Session 1

1   C   1.8.21   RC
According to the passage, the British were making money from the international slave trade. America wanted to keep money away from the British, so they did not purchase slaves from Britain.

2   A   1.8.18   RC
The first paragraph of the passage states that this speech declared the end of slavery in America. Answer choice A is correct.

3   D   1.8.03   V
According to the passage, the great irony was that slaveholders realized that they did not want to be enslaved by the British. To continue to do so would be a contradictory action. Answer choice D describes the best meaning for the word *irony*.

4   C   2.8.13   VLW
This passage is a nonfiction passage. It describes historical events that really took place.

5   D   1.8.24   RC
This passage explains that the institution of slavery was declining long before Abraham Lincoln announced its official end.

6   C   2.8.01   LET
Tom learns about a princely lifestyle through books. According to the excerpt, he "began to act the prince, unconsciously."

7   D   2.8.05   LET
This passage is written in the third person. A third-person narrator is someone who is telling the story but is not in the story. Answer choice D is correct.

8   A   2.8.01   LET
Tom's friends began to admire him when his speeches and mannerisms became courtly. Answer choice A is best.

9   B   1.8.18   RC
Tom does not beg for more money because the laws against mendicancy are stringent. Answer choice B is correct.

10   C   1.8.11   RS
Tom begins to imagine himself as a prince who lives in a palace while he is lying in bed at night because his head is filled with Father Andrew's stories. Answer choice C is the best answer.

11   D   1.8.12   RS
According to the passage, more than sixty percent of today's women work outside of the home. The author of the passage tells you that it was strange for a mother to work in the 1950s. Answer choice D describes the biggest difference between families today and those of the past.

12   A   1.8.21   RC
The passage states that the problem with the "Cleaver ideal" is that not all families fit into this mold.

13   D   1.8.01   V
The author says that today's families simply don't attempt to fit into the old-fashioned stereotype. Diverse family types are more accepted today.

14   B   1.8.14   RC
The author describes the shift in the way women were viewed in society and thinks that this is because more women attended college during the 1960s.

15   A   2.8.13   VLW
You can tell that this passage is an essay because it presents the author's point of view without making the author a subject of the essay.

16   B   1.8.15   RC
The poem is about a little boy who is waiting to see the lamplighter.

17   C   2.8.08   LET
According to the first stanza, the lamplighter walks by at teatime. Answer choice C is correct.

18   C   2.8.13   VLW
The passage is a poem. Answer choice C is the correct answer.

19   B   2.8.06   LET
The boy's tone is very excited when he talks about seeing the lamplighter.

20   A   1.8.05   V
This is the time of night they look out the window for the lamplighter.

21   B   1.8.11   RS
According the second paragraph, the Sumerians built magnificent burial chambers for their kings because they thought they were gods.

22   C   1.8.14   RC
According to the fourth paragraph, Queen Puabi's tomb was special because it was discovered still intact. Answer choice C is the best answer.

23   **D**   **1.8.18**   **RC**

According to the third paragraph, some people sacrificed themselves in the tomb so that they could serve the kings and queens in the afterlife.

24   **B**   **1.8.19**   **RC**

According to the passage, the queen's body was covered with a beaded cape. Answer choice B is correct.

25   **C**   **1.8.21**   **RC**

According to the second paragraph, common citizens were wrapped in a reed mat and buried.

26   **A**   **2.8.09**   **LET**

The narrator is fascinated with Antonia's actions and manners. The word *curiosity* best describes the narrator's attitude toward Antonia.

27   **C**   **2.8.01**   **LET**

The narrator comments that he doesn't think she should give her ring to someone she's just met.

28   **A**   **2.8.01**   **LET**

After Mr. Shimerda shows the book to the narrator's grandmother, he asks her to please teach his daughter. Answer choice A is the best answer.

29   **B**   **2.8.09**   **LET**

Antonia asks several questions that imply that she wants to learn English. Answer choice B is correct.

30   **D**   **1.8.03**   **V**

Antonia moves her hands rapidly and without thought, so that the narrator can't tell what she wants. You can guess that the word *impulsively* means "rapid and without thought."

Session 2

31   **B**   **1.8.14**   **RC**

The author mentions several times in the article that the cost of establishing a colony in space is unbelievable. He believes that the money could be better spent elsewhere. Answer choice B is the best answer.

32   **A**   **1.8.18**   **RC**

The author says at the end of the article that Earth is a healthy planet and the number of humans on Earth is increasing, so it isn't necessary to establish a space colony to preserve the human race.

33   B   1.8.21   RC
The answer to this question is right in the passage. The author says that people living in a space colony would have to bring water from Earth.

34   B   1.8.01   V
When the author says that up until a few years ago people considered space colonization a wild science-fiction tale, he means that they thought it would never happen. Answer choice B is the best choice.

35   C   1.8.03   V
The prefix in- means "not." The word *hospitable* means "welcoming." Therefore, the word *inhospitable* means "unwelcoming."

36   C   2.8.03   LET
Though all of the answer choices coincide with the author's view that people should not plan to live on Mars, at the end of the passage the author concludes that people should learn to behave more responsibly on planet Earth. Answer choice C is the best answer.

37   A   1.8.18   RC
The author explains that history has proved that nations have trouble working together and are often motivated by greed. He is concerned that nations working together to build a space colony will compete with each other.

38   C   1.8.12   RS
The answer to this question is right in the passage. The atmosphere on Mars is thinner than the atmosphere on Earth. Choice C is correct.

39   C   2.8.10   LET
Answer choice C contains repetition of initial consonant sounds in the words "humans," "have," "hatred," and "horror."

40   B   1.8.19   RC
You won't find the answer to this question in the passage. You have to draw a conclusion using information in the passage. The author says that even the world's finest scientists are still baffled by the question of how to keep people safe on another planet. This means that their knowledge is limited. Answer choice B is correct.

41   B   1.8.21   RC
The answer to this question is right in the passage. The author says that space colonists could regain some of the money spent on establishing a colony by mining for minerals. Answer choice B is the correct answer.

42   B   1.8.21   RC
The author writes that the estimated cost of a trip to Mars would be $30 billion. Answer choice B is correct.

43   C   1.8.03   V

In this part of the passage, the author is telling how humans might bring war and hatred to the new planet. When he says that would be "abominable," he means it would be terrible.

44   A   1.8.21   RC

One possible reason for going to Mars is to ensure the survival of the human race. However, the author believes humanity's survival isn't in danger because the Earth is still a healthy planet.

45   C   1.8.11   RS

Starting mines on Mars would cause people's greed to take over, and competition between companies to endanger the project. Answer choice C is correct.

46   B   2.8.13   VLW

This passage is an informational passage that expresses the author's personal opinions on the subject of space colonization. It is an essay.

47   **Extended Response   1.8.06   RS**

Sample answer: I agree with the author that a Mars colony would not benefit people. First of all, the author's point about our planet being perfectly good is very true. If humans invested a small amount of money or effort into cleaning up our world, it would serve us for many thousands of years to come. It would be wrong to grab more land without caring for what we have now. Additionally, Mars colonization would invite greed and conflict between nations. Throughout history, powerful nations have fought one another for control of 'new' places, and this would likely be no different. I think we should stay on Earth and make it as good as we can.

48   C   1.8.21   RC

The passage tells you that clean water is needed for the aquarium. The general guideline is that the water should be clean enough to drink.

49   A   1.8.23   RC

In the passage, the author explains that rocks and plants are optional add-ons for an aquarium. They are not items you need. Choice A is the best answer.

50   B   2.8.13   VLW

This is an instructional nonfiction passage. The other answer choices describe different types of fictional passages. Answer choice B is correct.

51   D   1.8.25   RC

These instructions deal with the general topic of setting up an aquarium. Water heaters and pumps each have specific directions for installation. Answer choice D is best.

Session 3

52   B   1.8.19   RC
Martha feels that the fresh air has made Mary look better. She doesn't comment on Mary's personality, though that has changed as well. The correct answer is B.

53   A   1.8.03   V
Even if the reader doesn't know the meaning of the word, they can look at the other words in the sentence to figure out the meaning. By looking at the other words in the sentence and the sentences that precede and follow it, the reader can see that the word means "wonderful." Answer choice A is correct.

54   B   2.8.03   LET
The passage focuses on the coming of spring and its renewing and healing powers. Mary looks better after spending time outdoors and thinks that Colin might, too. The narrator also comments that, as spring comes, the world looks as if something magical has happened to it.

55   C   1.8.19   RC
By looking at the rest of the passage, you can see that Mary has gone through a lot of changes. After looking at all the possible answers to this question, it is easy to see that only choice C relates to Mary's attitude.

56   C   2.8.05   LET
The narrator of this story is writing from a limited omniscient point of view. You can tell this because the narrator only reveals Mary's thoughts, and not the thoughts of the other characters.

57   B   1.8.16   RC
By looking at the answer choices, one should be able to decide which talks about the main idea and which are details found within the passage. The main idea is that she sees how much the garden has done for her and thinks Colin would feel better if he went out there too. Therefore, the correct answer choice is B.

58   D   2.8.06   LET
Colin tells Mary that he didn't scream when she walked in because he thought she was a ghost or a dream and "You can't bite a ghost or a dream, and if you scream they don't care." Therefore, choice D is the correct answer.

59   C   1.8.18   RC
The last paragraph tells the reader that the rain has done strange things to the garden. Answer choice C is best.

60   A   1.8.19   RC
In the beginning of the passage, we are told that it has been raining for days, and later that the rain has done strange things to the garden. The other choices are not mentioned in the passage. Therefore, the correct answer is A.

61   A   2.8.09   LET
There is no evidence in the passage that could lead the reader to believe that Mary is Colin's tutor. Also, there is also nothing that could support the idea that the two are siblings or cousins. Therefore, the correct answer choice is A.

62   A   1.8.24   RC
The passage is a fictional story. This means that the author is probably not trying to educate readers about gardens or inform them about how plants grow. There are no persuasive techniques in the passage. The author is writing to entertain.

63   B   1.8.03   V
Without knowing the meaning of the word, you can figure out that the word is similar to the word "opening" by looking at the clues in the sentence. You can also guess that the flower is not moving or falling, and you probably know that most flowers open in the spring, not close. Choice B is best.

64   C   1.8.19   RC
Colin tells Mary that he has always hated when people looked at him because they stare at him. He never says that people are afraid of him, or that they make fun of him, or that they laugh at him. Therefore, choice C is the correct answer.

65   B   1.8.19   RC
Mary says that she wants to know if Colin can be trusted because she wants to take him to the garden. He already knows about India and about Dickon. There is no mention of Mary's parents in the passage. The correct answer is B.

66   Extended Response   1.8.06   RS
Sample answer: I think that Mary will take Colin to the garden because she believes it will make him feel better. She thinks it will give him something to think about besides dying, and she probably doesn't want to listen to him talk about dying all of the time. She also wants to spend time outside because it is spring, and she might feel bad if she left Colin inside all alone, so she will probably share her secret with Colin and take him to the garden.

67   B   1.8.21   RC
The passage states that the stables are located on camp grounds. This makes it easy for interested campers to ride horses. Answer choice B is correct.

68   D   1.8.08   RS
The author has included the map to show the reader the layout of the camp. Therefore, choice D is the right answer.

69 **D** **1.8.24** **RC**

The purpose of this passage is to let people know what the camp is like. It lists all of the different components of the camp so that readers can learn about it. Choice D is the correct answer.

70 **B** **1.8.03** **V**

The sentence mentions the summer heat. It presents Camp Wallabe as an alternative to the heat. You can guess that the word *stifling* is related to feeling uncomfortable in the heat. The word *roasting* best fits this description. Answer choice B is the best answer.